One Common Enemy

Jim McLoughlin was born in Liverpool in
1921. He joined the Royal Navy at 17, serving
aboard the battleship HMS *Valiant* during the
Norwegian and Mediterranean campaigns. In
1955 Jim emigrated to South Australia, where
he and his wife Dorothy raised five children.

David Gibb is a writer with an abiding interest
in the literature of the Second World War,
especially the personal experiences of veterans.
He has worked extensively as a writer-producer
in the electronic and print media, and has had
short stories and poetry published. David lives
in Adelaide and is married to Chris, with whom
he has a son.

ONE COMMON ENEMY

The *Laconia* Incident: a survivor's memoir

Jim McLoughlin

with David Gibb

First published in the UK in 2006 by the National Maritime Museum,
Greenwich, London, SE10 9NF
www.nmm.ac.uk/publishing

First published in 2006 by
Wakefield Press, Adelaide, Australia

ISBN-10: 0 948065 77 X
ISBN-13: 978 0 948065 77 4

© Jim McLoughlin and David Gibb, 2006

1 2 3 4 5 6 7 8 9

A CIP catalogue record for this book is available from the British Library.

Text designed and typeset by Ryan Paine, Wakefield Press
Printed in China at Everbest Printing Co Ltd

Front cover: *Laconia* survivors being rescued
Back cover: *Laconia* survivors on the deck of U-156
(Photographs: Horst Bredow, U-boot Archiv)

Dedicated with an ocean of love to my wife Dorothy,

who wisely prefers to live in the present.

—J. M.

The Naval Hymn

Eternal Father, strong to save,
Whose arm doth bind the restless wave,
Who bidst the mighty ocean deep
Its own appointed limits keep:
O hear us when we cry to Thee
For those in peril on the sea.

Contents

Introduction

I wanted to tell this story because people forget what war is, how terrible it is. They forget how many people are killed, how many families are wrecked. In particular, they forget that a great many who actually *survive* the terrors of war remain, in some way, prisoners of cruel memories for the rest of their days. I am one of those survivors who, to use a naval analogy, remains permanently anchored in a sea of memories. The passing of the years is supposed to blunt the memory and yet, where these events are concerned at least, I find the opposite to be the case. They have become sharper and consequently more painful.

I am over 80 years old now, and much of what I relate here happened when I was in my late teens and early 20s. More than 60 busy years have gone by, yet there is never a day when I don't think of these events. And rarely a night when I am not more than a little unsettled by them. I can't forget what happened. These days I tend to forget some of the things I want to remember, yet remember a great many I'd rather forget. It's difficult and I believe I'll always struggle with it. Fortunately my strong faith has sustained me.

The events and conversations I've recorded here are based on my personal recollections. Many other *Laconia* survivors remember the same chaotic experience in ways that are unique to them. Like me, however, they remain haunted by memories.

Jim McLoughlin,
Adelaide, South Australia

Prologue
Many happy returns

Another day dawns and I know it's going to be like all the others. Nothing different. Nothing remarkable. I know that when it's over it will simply slip away and blur into all the other dreadful days we've already endured. I'm too bone weary to even think about what will happen next. And besides, I already know. Today, more of us will die in this wretched lifeboat.

The boat is 30 feet long and painted grey. It's really a very big rowing boat made of timber. A clinker hulled, open-whaler type of boat. A dirty sheet of yellow canvas is hanging motionless on an oar that the bosun erected as a makeshift mast. We're drifting on a calm sea, going God knows where. And going there slowly.

'What day is it?' a weak voice croaks unexpectedly, without any real interest, as if there is no particular need to know. It's a question asked for the sake of asking, an idle curiosity. I wonder what difference it could possibly make, knowing the date.

'It's October the second,' someone answers after I've forgotten the question. But the words send a signal into my jellied brain, a faint pinprick of recognition.

October the second. I know that date. I connect it to the year, 1942. Suddenly it makes sense.

'It's my birthday,' I announce, surprised at my own discovery. Then I think to add: 'My twenty-first birthday.'

There is a long silence. Eventually the British nurse, who is sitting near me, says: 'Well, that calls for a celebration.' Her smile, as always, makes me feel better. It gives me hope.

There is a strange stirring around me that I don't immediately connect with the announcement of my birthday. Then I see something being passed along from person to person, unsteady hand to unsteady hand. And then I'm holding it, looking at it rather stupidly. It's an oblong ration tin. Sparkling in the bottom is an unbelievably precious and generous gift of two tantalising tablespoons of water. A double ration. Because I'm 21.

I tilt the tin so the water runs into one corner, and fool myself into believing that I've been given even more than a double ration. I bring the tin to my lips and drink my birthday present, one jealously guarded sip after another, stretching out the moment, willing it not to end. But it does. The tin is empty. And that's my party. Over before it even begins. No one sings Happy Birthday. No one suggests I'm a jolly good fellow. No one has the strength.

I look around me. This is a very strange place to be spending my birthday, in a lifeboat somewhere in the Atlantic with a most peculiar bunch of party guests. They seem to have come in tattered fancy dress decorated with encrusted salt. Their lips are grotesquely swollen and split. Their faces are festooned with ugly strips of peeling skin.

How odd that there are mostly old people at my birthday party, and all uninvited come to think of it. More people should have been here today, but they've gone. Some left willingly. Others, I'm not so sure.

The morning is already hot, and I know it will get hotter. The sea looks oily, slick and unfriendly. The only thing on it is this lifeboat, and as my mind fades in and out of reality I become convinced that the world I once knew was nothing more than a figment of my imagination, that there has only ever been this boat and this place. We are deserted souls adrift on a deserted sea on a deserted planet. The loneliness is appalling. I'm now certain this dreadful isolation will be the death of me. If the sea isn't the death of me first.

Will I get to be 22? I can't concentrate long enough to answer my own question. In a strange way I don't care about my own suffering, but I worry greatly that my family will be tortured by grief when they hear of my fate. Perhaps they've been told already, told I'm dead when I'm not. Not yet, anyway. The thought of causing them anguish grinds away at my insides, doubling the dull ache of hunger.

How did I come to be here? What twists and turns of fate brought me to this moment, to this unknown spot in the Atlantic, to this sad and desperate little boat?

I know the answer to this only too well. I'm here because of Liverpool. Liverpool and the ships. It was always the magic of the ships pulling me to this point. I couldn't have resisted even if I'd tried.

1

Down among the ships

I was born on 2 October, 1921, in Walton, a grimy suburb just a few miles from the Liverpool docks. That's where I fell in love with ships and grew up with my brother George and sisters Florence, Dorothy and Enid. I was the second eldest. Our mother and father, Lillian and Benjamin, were kind, hard-working people who brought us up well in difficult times, in a city hit hard by unemployment during the Great Depression of the early 1930s.

We lived in a four-roomed terrace house in a dead-end street called Stepney Grove. It looked just like *Coronation Street*. A railway line ran past the back of our house and everything was forever covered in soot.

My father was in the merchant marine. He worked for the famous Cunard & White Star Line, as a first-class steward on the Atlantic run to New York. He wasn't around that much. He would come home about once every three or four weeks, stay for a few days, and then go to sea again. My mother, brother and three sisters were therefore the centre of my life. But it was my father and his work on the ships that influenced me most profoundly. It stirred me deep inside when he told me about his experiences at sea. Before he joined Cunard he had been with the Canadian Pacific Line for a time, and did a voyage to Sydney in 1931.

'They're building a huge bridge there,' he told me. 'It's like a big coat-hanger.'

'How can a bridge be like a coat-hanger, then?' I was fascinated by the idea that a bridge in far off Australia could resemble something as mundane as a coat-hanger in a cupboard in Liverpool.

'It's the same shape as a coat-hanger, a beautiful arch stretching out from opposite sides of the harbour. We sailed right under it,' he said. 'It's not finished yet, so there was a gap in the middle.'

I hung on every word. I thought he had the most exciting job in the world.

My father loved the Cunard liners, which he called 'his' ships. They had wonderfully evocative names like *Franconia*, *Laconia*, *Aquatania* and *Berengaria*, and carried people who lived, as he put it, 'on the other side'. He didn't mean the other side of the Atlantic either, rather the other side of prosperity from the one we were on.

It was impossible to grow up in Liverpool without being acutely aware of the docks and ships. Liverpool was a city of ships back then, the second largest port in Britain after London. The docks were like a magnet forever tugging at me. I just wanted to muck about down there more than anything else. My parents couldn't afford to buy us bikes, so I either walked or caught the tram, which cost one penny return. I can still remember the yellow ticket stub. The tram would take me down to Pier Head and the Landing Stage, a huge pontoon on the water, right in front of the famous Cunard Building. The liners used to come alongside it to disembark their passengers and I'd usually be there to watch the hustle. People who had been in New York only days ago would brush past me. It was absolutely marvellous.

There were always lots of cargo ships down at the docks too, loading and unloading. The docks ran for seven miles along the Liverpool waterfront. Staggering to think of it now. Everything was big, noisy and dirty. It smelt of the sea and rope tar and burnt sugar. It was a dangerous place for a child to be, but I didn't notice. To me it was an intoxicating kind of pandemonium, with cranes swinging huge cargo nets overhead, often bulging with bales of wool all the way from Australia. There were horse-drawn carts, lorries and tractor engines swarming all over the place and an elevated railway ran the length of the docks. Electric passenger trains rattled along it, bringing people down to the ships and the dockside factories. It was pretty rough, and risky too, but I couldn't get enough of it. It was a fantastic place for a boy to be.

One of the best things about the docks was that my mates and I could talk to the tough men who crewed the cargo ships. There were always blokes leaning over the railings, smoking cigarettes and watching the goings on below on the wharf. We'd call out to them and they'd reply in accents from all over the world.

'Where you from, mister?'

'South America.'

'That's a long way.'

'Very long way.'

'What's your cargo?'

'Sugar.'

'Where you taking it?'

'Maybe Canada, maybe Japan.'

'You got anything to eat?'

We would often try our luck asking for food because stooging around there all day made us awfully hungry. Occasionally they'd toss half a sandwich for us to fight over. Sometimes, though, those hard, haggard men would simply tell us to bugger off.

On summer nights it would be light until nearly 10 o'clock. It must have worried my mother terribly when I'd come home well after dark.

'Where have you been?' she'd ask.

'Down the docks.'

'How many times have I told you not to go there?'

Countless times, of course, but I couldn't help it. Those ships were in my blood, like a strange virus sailing through me.

Those innocent days on the docks with my tight-knit gang of mates were wonderfully happy. When we weren't hanging around in the shadows of ships we'd be fighting with some other gang, throwing stones and getting into harmless mischief. It was just boisterous boyhood fun. One of our favourite tricks was to annoy the local shopkeepers by throwing stones at the goods they had on display in front of their stores. The most inviting target was always stacked boxes of Woodbine cigarettes. Urging each other on, we'd lob stones from the other side of the street until the stack went sprawling over the footpath. Then we'd hide and watch as the angry shop owner came running out.

Sometimes we'd go into a biscuit shop to ask our favourite question.

'Got any broken biscuits, mister?'

'Yes.'

'Well why don't you mend 'em then?'

With that we'd run out of the shop laughing hysterically. We were the funniest people we knew.

Mum had a pretty good idea of what was going on, as mothers do, and occasionally she'd give me a stern reminder of exactly how far I could go.

'Don't you ever do anything that will bring a policeman to my door,' she warned.

But those pranks were only a minor distraction. Ships were what really mattered to me. Two in particular left a lasting impression on me, and helped shape my desire to go to sea. The first was Cunard's *Laconia*, my father's last ship before he came home from the sea forever. I treasured the thought that he worked and lived aboard this beautiful passenger liner for weeks at a time. She was an elegant ship and when I think of her now it is still with strong feelings of nostalgia.

Laconia was built in Scotland, at Wallsend-on-Tyne, in 1922, the year after I was born. She was 624 feet long, displaced nearly 20,000 tons, and steamed at 17 knots. She could accommodate 2000 passengers, which was only 500 fewer than the *Titanic*, which had been more than twice *Laconia*'s tonnage. Liverpool was her home port, so she mainly worked the Liverpool to New York route, although she also made a number of voyages from Hamburg to New York.

Because she was considered a ship of great luxury, *Laconia* was also in demand as a cruise ship, especially during the mid-1930s when the world had begun to crawl out from beneath the Depression. She cruised often to the West Indies and Madeira. Apart from her reputation as a fine cruise ship, she also claimed her place in nautical history by being the first passenger liner to circumnavigate the globe with the aid of a brand new invention called a gyro-compass. That was an astonishing achievement back then.

Laconia was built for the pleasure of those prepared to pay for comfort. When Dad took me aboard I was over-awed by the luxury I saw. It was a far cry from the way we all lived in Liverpool. There were glassed-in garden lounges with potted palms and exotic cane furniture, a verandah cafe, a library and writing room, a fashionable *salon*, a huge first-class dining room with marble pillars and, most oddly of all, a first-class smoking room which was a full-size replica of an old English inn, complete with its own massive open fireplace. Those luxuries stuck in my mind, but I can't say I took much notice of the lifeboats.

Even after my father left the sea for good in 1935 he still retained a strong connection to his last ship. One of our neighbours, a chap called Fred Eyres, was her chief pantry-man. When he and my father got together, their conversation was always about *Laconia*.

The other ship that inspired me was HMS *Royal Oak*, one of the Royal Navy's great Royal Sovereign Class battle-ships. A truly massive ship it was. Utterly huge. When I was 16, in the summer of 1938, *Royal Oak* paid a goodwill visit to Liverpool. I suspect now that the *real* aim was to recruit naive young chaps like me because Hitler was making loud noises over in Germany at that time.

The day *Royal Oak* was opened to the public in Liverpool

is still vivid in my mind. It seems impossible that it was more than 65 years ago. She was tied up at Gladstone Dock on a glorious summer's day, which was rare in Liverpool. A navy band was playing. Thousands of people were queuing and clamouring to get aboard her. Royal Navy sailors in crisp white uniforms were showing people around, pointing out the features of the ship, including the 15-inch guns on her foredeck. I was mesmerised. She was a magnificent ship, but dark and somehow sinister, built for war at sea. She had a beam of almost 90 feet and a vast superstructure that towered over her. It took a crew of 1200 men to sail her.

I was gone for all money. If the Royal Navy had tapped me on the shoulder I would have stayed aboard and set off that very day. It suddenly occurred to me, right there on the deck of *Royal Oak* with her flags fluttering in the breeze, that the best way to go to sea would be with the Royal Navy. My course was set.

To help contribute to the family finances, I had left school at 14 and found work. I delivered groceries on a bicycle for a time, and later worked on a horse-drawn laundry van, picking up and delivering washing. I loathed every second of those jobs because all I wanted was to go to sea. The idea of joining the navy grew bigger in my mind, right through to the end of 1938 and into 1939. By then I'd turned 17, and from time to time I would run into a lad I knew called Johnny McCormack. He had already joined the navy and whenever he came home on leave I was fascinated by his uniform and his jaunty, devil-may-care attitude. I wanted to be just like Johnny, so in March

1939 I went to the Royal Navy recruiting office near the Liverpool Docks and got the enlistment papers. I took them home for my parents to sign because I was too young to sign them myself.

'What's all this?' my mother asked.

'Papers for joining the Royal Navy.'

'That's no life, you know, being in the navy.' I made Mum very unhappy when I brought those papers home, but I think she knew it was inevitable. Going to sea was all I'd talked about.

'I'll see the world,' I said. 'It'll be fun.'

'You make your bed, you lie in it,' she said.

Dad, on the other hand, understood. He didn't try to talk me out of it. 'Is this what you really want?' he asked.

'Yes.' I was very firm about it.

'All right then.' And without saying anything more he signed the papers. So I joined the Royal Navy, signing on for seven years of service. Simple as that.

2

New mates and marmalade

A few weeks later, in April, I found myself at Lime Street Station waiting to catch a train south to Plymouth, clutching my Royal Navy travel warrant and wondering what I'd let myself in for. I'd never been beyond Liverpool before, not even to Manchester, a mere 30 miles away. Fortunately I found some unexpected moral support in three other worried lads waiting near me on the platform. I sidled over, they looked me up and down, saw my warrant, showed me theirs, and said hello.

'I'm Johnny Hennessey,' said one. 'What's your name?'

'Jim McLoughlin.'

'Hello, Mac,' Johnny said, then introduced me to the other lads, Charlie Hughes and Freddie Powell.

'Hello, Mac,' they said.

We all shook hands and from that moment I was known to my shipmates as Mac. We settled ourselves in the train and talked about nothing else but going to sea on warships. I was in good company.

We got off the train at Devonport, the largest naval dockyard in Britain, on the River Tamar near Plymouth, and walked up to the Royal Naval Barracks, called HMS *Drake*. This place was known as a 'stone frigate' because it was a shore establishment. It was our first hint that the

Royal Navy was really a world within a world, complete with its own mysterious customs and traditions.

From the moment we reported for duty it was made abundantly clear that, as new recruits with the service's lowest rank of ordinary seaman, the navy owned us completely. We were immediately put in the hands of a leading seaman instructor who showed us to our barracks and then saw to it that we were kitted out with our uniforms. He introduced us to each item of our kit.

'This is your cap, McLoughlin,' he said.

'Yes, sir.'

'Here are your sea boots, and that there is your duffle bag.'

'Thank you, sir.'

'Do you want a ditty box?'

'Do I want a what, sir?' I looked blankly at the leading seaman.

'A ditty box.' He produced a little wooden box with a hinged lid. 'It's to put your personal things in,' he explained.

'What sort of personal things, sir?'

'Do you have a mother?'

'Yes.'

'I'm surprised. But if your mother sends you a letter, you keep it in your ditty box, understand?' I nodded and he went on: 'If you have a photograph of your girlfriend, you keep that in your ditty box as well.'

'I'll have a ditty box, then,' I said, even though I didn't have a girlfriend, let alone a photograph of her.

We were each issued our own blanket, too. It was cream with a black stripe running across the top of it.

'See that black stripe?'

'Yes, sir.'

'Right. If I ever see a blanket that's gone the same colour as the black stripe, the owner will be in trouble. Cleanliness is next to godliness in the Royal Navy.'

'Yes, sir.'

We quickly discovered another tradition. Our uniform wasn't merely a uniform. It was a symbol. The big serge collar on our tunic had three narrow white stripes around it. Those three stripes, we were told, symbolised the three battles of Nelson. And the reason the collar draped over the shoulders and down between the shoulder blades dated from centuries ago when sailors wore their hair long and tied it back into a single tarred pigtail. The long collar prevented tar from soiling the tunic at the back.

We each received the standard navy hammock. It was like a big sausage that we had to learn to undo and hang in our allocated space in the barracks. That was the easy bit. The hard part was tying it all up again so it looked like a big sausage once more. It had to be done right or there was trouble. There wasn't an ordinary bed to be seen in our barracks. After a time we got used to the hammocks and found them quite comfortable.

Every morning at 5.30 sharp, our instructor would barge his way into the barracks and go along the line of hammocks, thumping them from underneath as he passed. 'Wakey wakey, rise and shine! Show a leg!' he yelled.

His name was John Tennant. I've never forgotten this tough, uncompromising Liverpool man. He had us living in fear much of the time. To a bunch of raw 17-year-olds he seemed like an old salt, but he was probably only about 30.

Ten minutes after jolting us awake, Tennant would be back in the barracks to check if we had our hammocks stowed properly. Anyone who didn't was made to run out to the flagstaff on the parade ground with their hammock slung over a shoulder. The flagstaff was like a ship's mast, and just as high, with a yardarm near the top. Tennant would force hammock offenders to climb up one side of the flagstaff, clamber over the yardarm and make their way down the other side. The flagstaff was often wet and slippery first thing in the morning and there was a steel wire net round the bottom, a few feet off the ground.

'Don't slip!' Tennant would yell gleefully.

'No, sir.'

'If you fall onto that net you'll come through the other side looking like potato chips!'

'Yes, sir.'

I didn't fancy that at all, so my hammock was always among the first to be properly stowed away each morning. Later on we all had to climb that flagstaff and it wasn't for the faint-hearted.

Another unique custom of the navy was its language. We started off saying 'Yes, sir' but were soon indoctrinated into using the navy version: 'Aye aye, sir'. We learnt that we didn't call the Royal Navy the Royal Navy, even though that's what it was. We referred to it as the Andrew after Lieutenant Andrew Miller, a member of Portsmouth's notorious 'Press Gang' who once claimed he owned the Royal Navy because of the huge number of men he 'pressed' into its service during the late 18th century. We didn't call the sea the sea, either, even though that's what it was. We called it the drink. And we didn't go to the toilet anymore. We went to the heads. Even our leading seaman's early morning wake-up call was a tradition dating back to the 17th century, when sailors' wives or girlfriends were permitted to sleep on board when their ship was in harbour. When the shout 'Show a leg!' was heard, the ladies would display a stocking-clad leg to indicate their presence in a sailor's hammock, where they could stay for a further 30 minutes while the men got up to start work. Soon navy-speak became second nature to us.

The first part of our five-month training course involved long sessions of parade-ground drill. They really hammered it into us, that drill business, and there was always plenty of shouting going on. We had to do it perfectly, so we did it over and over again. It taught us discipline and how to work in harmony as a group. Discipline and loyalty, that's what it was all about, and those values have helped me through my life ever since. We spent hours in the classroom each day, too, learning the theory of seamanship, knots and splicing and all that. We studied history, geography and mathematics as well because the navy demanded that we acquire a broad education. For a time it felt like I'd gone back to school, except that I was in uniform.

I especially enjoyed the company of my classmates. We became close because we all wanted the same thing, to go to sea. But I did have one bitter disagreement, and that was over something petty: a tin of marmalade jam.

'Pass the marmalade, Hicks,' I said to a classmate, a lad from the north of England. We were sitting at our mess table having a meal.

'When I've finished with it.'

'When will that be, then?'

'When I've finished with it, that'd be when.'

I waited a while. Hicks wasn't digging any more jam out of the tin.

'Finished with the marmalade, Hicks?'

'No.'

'Yes you have.'

'No I haven't.'

We went on like that for a bit, then I lost my temper. I lunged at him across the table and before I knew it we were brawling, gripping each other by the tunic. Eventually our classmates intervened and we cooled down. I loved marmalade, still do as it happens, and from that day on, Hicks and I barely spoke.

Eventually our instructors began to introduce us to the sea and ships. We went out on the River Tamar in rowing boats to learn the basics of seamanship. They taught us to row, which I enjoyed. It was hard work, but I liked the feel of it as we pulled on the oars as a crew, with an instructor up in the bow calling out the rhythm.

'In, pull, out, feather, in, pull, out, feather, in . . .'

We went on board the Royal Navy vessels that were tied up in the Devonport Dockyards. I loved that. Our instructors explained the functions of the various parts of a ship, the mess decks, the bridge, the gun stations, as well as all the traditional ways of behaving on board, what to do, what not to do. It was orientation, I suppose. One day, though, they took us aboard a submarine. I didn't like that at all. I couldn't think why anyone would want to be cooped up hundreds of feet beneath the surface. I couldn't get off quick enough. Being introduced to those ships made us all feel that we were becoming sailors at last, but we seemed no closer to going to sea.

Then we began to learn about gunnery and signalling and electrics and torpedoes and wireless telegraphy, a little bit of everything to give us a broad picture of all the Royal Navy trades so that, when we finished our basic training, we could weigh up our options.

'Maybe I'll be a wireless telegrapher,' I said.

'Yeah, that'd be okay I suppose,' Johnny replied.

'What about signals?' Charlie asked. 'You'd get to know everything that was going on if you were in signals.'

'One thing's for sure,' I said, 'there's no way I'm going to be a stoker.'

'No one wants to be a bloody stoker,' Freddie said. 'I'm going to stay an ordinary seaman. That way you get to work the guns.'

'Now that'd be something, that would.'

'Imagine firing one of those big 15-inch buggers!'

'I'll be in that. It's ordinary seaman for me, then.'

The four of us had become inseperable by that stage, so there and then I decided to remain an ordinary seaman, too. I suppose I didn't have much ambition. I just wanted to get to sea on a ship with my mates.

We finished our basic training course toward the end of August 1939 and for a few days we hung around HMS *Drake* waiting impatiently to be drafted to a ship. Then, on the afternoon of 3 September, we were sitting in the mess listening to the radio when Prime Minister Neville

Chamberlain announced that Britain had declared war on Germany. We were pretty excited when we heard that. We could finally put to sea and get stuck into a real war.

This is more like it.

I didn't have a clue what war meant, so it just seemed like the start of a fantastic adventure when my mates and I were drafted to the aircraft carrier HMS *Courageous*. We couldn't stop smiling. But *Courageous* was already at sea and, because the war had started, she couldn't turn around just so we could join her, so our draft was cancelled almost straight away. We were shattered. We continued to hang around *Drake* until one afternoon we heard on the mess radio that *Courageous* had been torpedoed. The loss of life was huge, but it didn't affect me at all. Not one iota.

Well, that was a bit lucky.

In mid-October we heard that *Royal Oak*, the battleship that had so influenced me to join the Royal Navy, had been torpedoed by a German U-boat while moored in the apparent safety of her anchorage at Scapa Flow in Scotland. They said she'd blown up, rolled over and gone down in just 13 minutes. She came to rest on her side in 90 feet of water with 800 sailors trapped inside. I'd been on board her just the year before, so I found that news a bit sobering.

But it won't happen to me.

After leave in November, my draft finally came through. With my three close mates, and indeed most of my class-mates, I was going to HMS *Valiant*. She was a Queen Elizabeth Class battleship of more than 30,000 tons, a marvellous and powerful ship armed with eight 15-inch guns and twenty 4.5-inch guns. She had a top speed of 24 knots.

I was thrilled about being drafted to *Valiant* because she was newly recommissioned after a major reconstruction, so was like a brand new ship.

It was a cold, wet evening when I joined the ship in Devonport. It was 26 November 1939 and I had a hammock slung over my shoulder and a duffle bag in the other hand as I walked up the gangway. There was confusion everywhere. Nobody seemed to know what was going on, which is the way it often appears when a big warship is being made ready for sea. It's organised chaos.

I was 18 years old and couldn't believe my luck.

3

Valiant days

I went below and was immediately lost. HMS *Valiant* was vast, with multiple decks and a dizzying network of companionways and stairs that all looked the same to me. I couldn't tell whether I was facing the bow or stern, port or starboard. I only started to get my bearings when we were allocated quarters according to our trades. Seamen here, stokers over there, wireless operators/telegraphers, shipwrights, cooks and clerks each to their separate mess decks in various parts of the ship. Those for the ordinary seamen were two decks down, deep in the bow of the ship.

Johnny, Charlie and Freddie went starboard, while I was sent to the port mess. It certainly wasn't designed for comfort: four or five big tables, storage racks for hammocks, some stools, a few crockery shelves, and not much else. After the routine of life ashore at HMS *Drake*, I felt confused and alone in my new mess as I watched a parade of strange faces and heard the bedlam of unfamiliar voices. What was what? Who was who? It felt unreal starting a new job in what was also my new home. And I wasn't exactly thrilled when I learnt that John Tennant, our hard-nosed leading seaman from HMS *Drake* was in charge of my mess. I'd have to keep my wits about me if I was going to stay out of trouble. That first night I went to sleep in my hammock with mixed feelings. I was excited to be on my first ship, yet fearful that I'd make an idiot of myself in front of the sea-hardened members of the crew.

Next day we were each shown to the part of the ship we would be working in. My station was on the quarterdeck, where all the officers were.

'You'll be a lookout up on the bridge,' I was told.

God, just my luck, surrounded by officers and nowhere to hide.

Later, the ranks of the Royal Navy would swell with officers who signed on only for the duration of hostilities. Until then, though, *Valiant* was commanded by long-serving career officers. From the captain down to the petty officers, they were seasoned hard-liners, intent on doing everything by the book. The captain was H B Rawlings, a very tall, gaunt man with a sunburnt face who had that stern, superior look of command about him.

We were taken to our action stations. Mine was in the third 4.5-inch gun turret on the port side.

Now, this is more like it.

I couldn't have been happier. There was one small problem, though. Hicks, the bloke I'd fought with over the tin of marmalade, was assigned to the same gun crew. Still, there were more important things to think about than the chilly tension that lingered between us.

With our stations sorted out, we were given our first shipboard duty: painting *Valiant*'s entire top deck grey. Under war conditions there was no longer a place for the traditional white decks and polished brass fittings so loved by the navy in peacetime. The duller we could make it, the safer the ship would be, apparently. So I spent my first couple of days aboard *Valiant* on my knees, paintbrush in hand, applying lashings of grey paint to the deck. It wasn't quite the glamorous start I'd imagined.

Three days later the ship slipped away from Devonport without fanfare and crept into Plymouth Sound, where she anchored and made final preparations. No one told us where we were going. All we knew was that we would soon be commencing *Valiant*'s working-up trials, when everything on the ship, including the crew, would be repeatedly tested with ever-increasing intensity to ensure her readiness for war. But there *was* someone who seemed to know a great deal more than us. His name was William Joyce, the notorious British fascist who, when war broke out in September, had fled to Germany and started broadcasting propaganda programs back to Britain. Spouting information provided by German spies in Britain, he was loathed by his listeners, who nicknamed him Lord Haw Haw for his high-pitched, upper-class English accent.

Remarkably, our captain allowed Lord Haw Haw's weekly ravings to be played over *Valiant*'s loudspeaker system, known as the tannoy. We'd hear a sharp click as the tannoy came alive, there'd be a brief hiss of static, and then an exaggerated plum-in-the-mouth voice would try to put the wind up us.

'Oh, I see that HMS *Valiant* is making ready to go to sea now,' Lord Haw Haw would say. 'Well, we'll be waiting for you when you get out to sea, boys.'

'Bullshit!' we would yell in unison, and follow up with cheers, whistles and crude insults.

'We'll be watching everything you do. Absolutely every-thing,' the traitor said.

'Bullshit! Turn the bastard off!'

We thought it was hilarious. No way was he going to frighten a bunch of 18-year-olds about to sail off on their first great adventure. We dismissed Joyce as a fool who'd chosen the wrong side. Apprehension lurked in each of us, though. But it was just butterflies in the stomach. There wasn't any fear.

At last the great moment came. Shepherded by a reassuring group of destroyers, we steamed out of Plymouth Sound one night into the English Channel, heading west into the unknown. I was on duty with five other lookouts on the bridge as we went out. I couldn't believe it. Only a few months before I'd been at home in Liverpool, living an ordinary life with my family. Then I was off to war on the bridge of one of the Royal Navy's most powerful ships, rugged up in a seaman's duffle coat with a pair of binoculars glued to my eye sockets. And goodness, was I keyed up! As the ship's lookouts we had to report absolutely everything we saw, and woe betide us if the officers on the bridge spied something before we did. So there was an endless stream of calls from the lookouts.

'Bearing red two zero five, a light,' someone reported. That was probably a buoy in the channel.

'Bearing green zero nine zero, a headland.'

'Bearing green one seven five, a fishing smack.' Although the war had started, the fishermen were still out there working in their little boats, braving the Channel at night.

And so it went on.

'Bearing red two seven zero. A fun fair.' Stunned silence followed that report from a young seaman called Glover. He was about my age.

'A what?' an incredulous officer demanded at last.

'One very big fun fair, sir. Bearing red two seven zero, sir,' Glover repeated. A stifled snigger or two rippled around the bridge.

'I think you'll find, seaman, that it's a neutral ship with all its lights on,' came the officer's exasperated reply.

'Aye aye, sir. A ship with lights, sir.' I was relieved it was Glover who'd made a fool of himself and not me. Still, it was early days. Before long we became accomplished observers, our confidence rising as we settled into life on board our great battleship.

As we left the Channel and steamed into the Atlantic, the tempo of ship life grew faster. We were busy all the time, with every station on high alert, especially for submarines. They were the big worry, it seemed to me, and even as *Valiant* made her way westwards, our destroyer escort would occasionally drop a brace of depth charges. There'd be huge explosions as they detonated below the surface, sending up massive spouts of water. All false alarms. We took all this in our stride after a while as we slipped into the routine of our four-hour watches.

I was always dog tired when I stumbled off my watch, too tired even to unroll my hammock and hang it in the mess. I didn't bother. I got into the habit of sleeping on a stool in the corner, tin helmet on my head and gas mask at the ready on my lap. I found it quite comfortable and far more convenient. It saved time because I didn't have to worry about stowing and unstowing my hammock all the time. Besides, if we came under attack, I wanted to get to my action station fast.

There was still no word over the tannoy about where we were going. The tannoy's click, hiss and crackle began to make us nervous. We never knew what was coming. Often it was a bugle call, with different calls for action stations, air raids, colours and so on. Sometimes it was just a routine announcement of some kind. But eventually the words we'd been waiting for were broadcast throughout the ship.

'Captain speaking,' came the voice of command. 'We are proceeding for our working-up trials and our destination is Bermuda.'

The captain then told us what needed to be improved aboard *Valiant*. Our general preparedness was good, but we would have to be much faster getting to action stations. He reminded us that we were at war, which seemed to be stating the obvious. But at least we knew where we were going.

This is all right. My first ship in the Royal Navy and I'm off to sunny Bermuda. Sounds pretty nice to me.

But the work on board grew even more demanding as the ship and her crew went through their paces. Exercises went on, day and night. Calls to fire stations. Calls to action stations. Everything was done under the stopwatch and the officers were never satisfied. We had to do it faster, they said. Always faster, always better, always reminding us that there was a war on.

When they called 'Action stations!' I would have to bolt from the bridge and fly down a series of steep stairs to reach my turret on the port side. But while I was going down, hordes of other seamen were going up to their action stations, so everyone was jostling and bumping into everyone else in this mad scramble to beat the clock and please the captain.

With all the drills, we had precious little time to ourselves. But there were moments when I could just stand out on deck and watch the sea. It was incredibly beautiful, no matter what the weather was like, and I was awed by the power of the waves and the spectacular sunsets. Seen from the deck of a ship many hundreds of miles from the nearest land, those fiery sunsets were an unforgettable sight. I loved being out there with the sea all around me. I loved every moment of it.

On one occasion as part of our ongoing training, we were allowed what was called 'a trick on the wheel', the naval term for steering a ship. *Valiant* wasn't steered from the bridge, but from a small room directly below it that was lit only by dim red lights. It took a while for the eyes to adjust to their eerie glow. A group of us were given our trick on the wheel under the critical eyes of the chief quartermaster and the chief petty officer, and my goodness it was a delicate business. The wheel was about the size of a car steering wheel and we had to steer the ship on the exact heading called down from the bridge by the officer of the watch. I was all over the place like a mad woman's custard. I couldn't keep *Valiant* on the required heading for more than a few seconds. The trick, it seemed, was to start the ship turning onto the required heading, then bring the wheel in the opposite direction almost straight away.

This anticipated the long delay between turning the wheel and the ship actually changing course. I went back to my watch on the bridge to an earful of sarcasm from the other young seamen.

'Was that you doing your trick just then, Mac?'

'Yes,' I said proudly.

'Well, we were pretty safe while you were down there.'

'Why's that?'

'You had us bloody zigzagging so much a submarine couldn't possibly have hit us.'

I just grinned and ignored them. I'd been steering one of the world's most powerful, complex machines. Not very well, but I'd steered it. Life was pretty damned good as far as I was concerned.

As we continued southwest across the Atlantic toward Bermuda, we sailed through the Saragossa Sea, an expanse of thick brown seaweed stretching from horizon to horizon. There seemed no end it. It flattened the sea so much it gave the impression that the ship was cleaving its way through solid land. *Valiant* took two days and nights to steam through this vast, gently heaving brown carpet.

We'd just put the eerie calm of the Saragossa behind us when a hurricane ripped the sea into a savage frenzy. I'll never forget it. We knew it was coming well enough, but that didn't prepare us for its ferocity. *Valiant* might have been a battleship of more than 30,000 tons but the waves treated her with contempt. She heaved, pitched, twisted and heeled over with unimaginable violence. I was hanging on for dear life on the bridge, and I had to stay up there after my watch had finished because it was too dangerous to move.

The view from the bridge fascinated and terrified me at the same time. Those waves were easily 70 or 80 feet high, perhaps even higher. Absolute monsters. *Valiant*'s bow would explode out of the water as she came shuddering off the top of a wave, then go careering down the other side into a seething trough. When we reached the bottom we'd look up and see the next wave looming and rushing toward us. It would crash on the bow, submerging the foredeck and the 15-inch guns, then come thundering directly at the bridge, a fearsome battering ram of grey-green water that seemed to stop the ship dead in her tracks. The noise was horrific, a nerve-piercing, relentless shriek like the world had gone mad. On the bridge we had to yell to each other to be heard. I was frightened out of my wits and wasn't alone in that.

Our escort of destroyers, all much smaller than *Valiant*, got pounded far worse than us and I've always been amazed that some of them didn't go down. With the towering waves breaking over them, if sea water had flooded in through their funnels they would have gone straight to the bottom. Eventually the destroyers had to leave us to our own devices and staggered off to safer waters. They eventually found refuge in New York. So there we were, totally unprotected in that awful hurricane, but its fury was probably our protector. A submarine would never have been able to attack us in those conditions. A sub would have to run deep beneath the turmoil while any German surface ships would find it impossible to bring their guns to bear on us. Eventually, after more than 24 hours of constant battering, we came out of the worst of it. The ship was chaotic inside.

We found the crockery in pieces across the mess deck and it took ages to get everything ship-shape again because the sea remained rough for a number of days.

During this rough spell I was taking my turn as cook. Just before lunch one day, I was carrying a tray full of prunes and custard down the stairs between the galley and the mess deck. The stairs were wet and so were the sea boots I was wearing, so I was a disaster waiting to happen. I had mastered the naval tradition of scurrying down the ship's steep and narrow stairs frontward, without hanging on to the side rails. This left the hands free for carrying trays of prunes and custard. However, this time my boots slipped from under me and I crashed to the mess deck, launching the prunes and custard on a horizontal trajectory that coincided perfectly with the arrival of the officer of the day as he passed the stairs. In an instant I was lying in an unprofessional heap on the deck, and the prunes and custard were decorating one side of the officer of the day's neatly pressed uniform. I was mortified, but he was a quiet, gentlemanly type, so he passed it off as an unfortunate rough-weather incident.

We were relieved to reach the tranquillity of Bermuda. As we steamed into Hamilton Harbour in brilliant sunshine, *Valiant* looked bedraggled with her superstructure damaged and her grey paint encrusted with salt. It looked like patches of snow had been dumped on her. An American cruise liner, the *President Roosevelt*, was berthed in the harbour. A cruise ship seemed strange to us in wartime, but of course America wasn't in the war yet. As we steamed by, her passengers lined the railings and cheered us. It gave us a good feeling, that did.

We lay up in Hamilton Harbour for a couple of days in mid-December while we licked our wounds and got *Valiant* ready for sea again, straightening damaged structures and tidying up the paintwork. I went ashore with my shipmates, too. In addition to Johnny, Charlie and Freddie, my mates from HMS *Drake*, I'd also teamed up with two other young sailors, a tall, skinny chap called Peter Rimmer and another lad truly called Davey Jones. Davey Jones was an ironical name for a seaman if ever I heard one, because of the age-old nautical reference to Davy Jones's Locker, the mythical place at the bottom of the ocean where all drowned sailors reside! The six of us went ashore together in Bermuda. There was something odd about the place.

'Notice anything?' I asked.

'I notice there are no beautiful girls rushing out to meet us,' Peter complained.

'Yeah, I noticed that as well,' Davey said.

'No, not that. Listen. There are no cars,' I remarked. The others listened and everyone agreed Bermuda was very quiet.

'No cars *and* no girls,' Johnny moaned.

That's the main thing I remember about Bermuda, apart from it being warm. There didn't seem to be any cars, only bicycles, which were everywhere. But it was quiet and peaceful, and the grim war mood of England seemed remote. Even though we'd had a few submarine alerts and heard the occasional *Boom! Boom!* of depth charges, the war hadn't touched us yet.

While we were in Bermuda, news came through that a German raider, the pocket battleship *Admiral Graf Spee*, was lurking in the South Atlantic off South America. We weren't an awfully long way from that ship, and I've often wondered since if the reason *Valiant* got sent in that general direction was in case the *Graf Spee* became a threat. As it turned out, the German ship was badly damaged in a fierce action against three British cruisers, which saw her withdraw to the harbour of Montevideo in Uruguay, where her crew scuttled her. We weren't called on to help our cruisers in that skirmish, so we left Bermuda and sailed up the east coast of America to Halifax, Nova Scotia, in Canada. We continued our working-up trials along the way, practicing our shipboard drills day and night, especially our gunnery. There was no let-up.

It was freezing in Halifax, snow and ice everywhere. Hard to take after balmy Bermuda. But the weather was calm, so we went ashore and walked about carefully on the icy streets. There were groups of pretty young girls skating on the roads, skylarking about. They called out to us cheekily, as young girls do when they see sailors. I went to a dance hall and saw people doing the jitterbug. I'd never seen or heard anything like it in England. It was terrific fun, so fast and full of life and utterly carefree.

From Halifax we joined a Canadian convoy as part of its escort to Britain. It was carrying food and other war supplies, I believe, and there were Canadian corvettes sailing with us in the escort group, too. We were on high-alert during that trip, crossing the Atlantic on the way back to England. The closer we got to home, the greater the threat from German submarines and aircraft. We weren't attacked and, even though we thought of ourselves as ready for war, I wasn't disappointed by the lack of action.

After we'd seen the Canadian ships safely to their ports, we continued on to Orkney in Scotland, joining the Home Fleet in Scapa Flow, where the poor old *Royal Oak* was lying on the bottom. We stayed there for what seemed like an eternity. It was a dismal place, Scapa Flow, cold, windswept and surrounded by bare hills. *Valiant*'s crew got bored up there with nothing to do except routine duties, painting and general maintenance. Sailors from other ships gave us a fair bit of mouth while we were lying idle. 'Big-ship sailors doing precious little,' they'd sneer at us, trying to start a fight.

There was always strong rivalry between the crews of big ships and small ships, but the Royal Navy wasn't about to risk a big battleship like *Valiant* unless there was serious work for her to do. So we sat there, ignoring the remarks, biding our time until, in February 1940 we became involved in the Norwegian Campaign, on escort duty mainly, coming and going from Scapa Flow in support of British operations off the Norwegian coast. We'd leave Scapa, sail past Shetland and continue to the Norwegian Sea, where life began to hot up.

The German ship *Altmark*, which had once been the *Graf Spee*'s supply ship, was known to be transporting 300 British merchant navy prisoners through neutral Norwegian waters to Germany. The prisoners were battened down below decks and Winston Churchill, who was still First Lord of the Admiralty at that early stage of the war, was having none of it. He ordered that the *Altmark* be boarded by force and the prisoners released, even though she was in neutral waters. So a raiding party was cobbled together from sailors of the various Royal Navy ships in the area, including *Valiant*.

There were many unforgettable characters on *Valiant*, believe me, but probably the most outrageous was a bloke in the mess next to mine. His name was Tom Cox, a huge, dark-complexioned man who'd been in the Royal Navy forever. He had a black beard and a moustache that curled up at both ends. He looked like a Spanish pirate and was without doubt *Valiant*'s most outstanding seaman. Whenever we had an air raid, Tom would go out on deck to scream abuse at the Germans flying overhead. 'Bugger off, you bastards!' he'd yell, shaking his fists at the enemy aircraft. He'd once been a petty officer but had been repeatedly demoted for various misdemeanours and was back to the rank of able seaman. But with his strength and ferocious appearance, he was a natural choice to represent our ship in the raiding party.

Tom, to our utter amazement, set off for this dangerous task armed only with a cutlass. After much violence on board the *Altmark*, the British prisoners were freed and the buzz went around that he'd played the leading role. We gaped as he climbed back on board our ship with his cutlass clenched between his teeth, swaggering a bit. He did it as a lark, to stir the officers up, but this extraordinary sight left a lasting impression on the teenage seamen like me. We thought he was larger than life, and more than a little frightening come to think of it. The officers despaired at Tom's undisciplined behaviour, but they were reluctant to get rid of him because he was so good at all he did.

In April, after the Germans had invaded Norway, we

were part of an escort for three liners carrying Britain's Guards Brigade to the little port of Harstad in Andifiord, the northern approach to Narvik above the Arctic Circle. The German battleship *Tirpitz* was known to be lurking in the fiords of Norway and it was our job to shield the troop-carrying liners.

I'll never forget the beauty of that fiord. We steamed into it in perfectly clear weather, blue skies, mirror-calm sea, snow shining on the tops of the mountains on either side. It was wonderful. We were in the land of the midnight sun, but even as I admired the beauty around me I was aware of the danger. What were we doing bringing a huge battleship into a fiord like this with land towering on either side, and only about an hour of twilight before it was day again?

This is crazy. Just plain crazy.

We had destroyers with us, which was reassuring, and also the aircraft carrier *Ark Royal* with its squadron of Skua dive-bombers. But the Germans had established air bases in Norway and if the Luftwaffe got to us we'd be hopelessly trapped. Like sitting ducks, we were, and I didn't much fancy being sunk. We'd been told if we ever ended up in the drink in the Arctic we'd be dead within three minutes.

Nothing came of it in the end. With the ship on high-alert, we went into the harbour at Harstad, the troops disembarked safely from the liners, and we came straight out again. But the possibility of air raids put us on edge, and gave us a taste of the tension we could expect as the war pushed on. After another stint at Scapa Flow, where it was still cold and boring, it was a great relief when we were ordered to join H Force at Gibraltar.

'There are monkeys in Gibraltar,' Charlie announced.

'Bollocks. You only get monkeys in Africa,' scoffed Freddie.

'You'll see I'm right soon enough,' Charlie countered. He was a cocky lad.

'One thing's for certain, there'll be a bunch of bloody ugly monkeys in Gibraltar when we get there,' Johnny decided.

'It'll be nice and warm, that's all I know,' I said.

'Yeah, a Mediterranean holiday, that's what we'll be having.'

We steamed south toward warmer waters and once the bitter cold of Scotland was well behind us we were issued with white uniforms and pith helmets. *Mad dogs and Englishmen, out in the midday sun!* Each day it got warmer and soon they put us on shorter watches, so we had more spare time than usual. We'd lie about on the deck near the big guns, stripped to the waist, soaking up the unfamiliar warmth of the sun. *This is okay, Gibraltar will be like Bermuda.*

Having time to lie about in the sun had its disadvantages, and they weren't confined to sunburn. There was too much time to think. The action in Norway showed me that war was a dangerous business and that I was well and truly in it, like it or not. I began to worry about my future as I realised that being in the Royal Navy meant more than adventure. *This could easily get me killed.* The anxiety was building and I'm sure my shipmates were having the same thoughts. But it wasn't the sort of thing we talked about as we steamed down the coast of Portugal and through the Straits of Gibraltar to the legendary British stronghold at the bottom of Spain.

Being in Gibraltar's harbour, in the shadow of that awesome rock, made us feel strangely secure. Soon after we arrived, the buzz around the mess deck was all about the Italian aircraft that were often seen flying high overhead.

'Those Italians, they can't bomb us while we're here, you know,' someone said. It was such an outlandish claim that it got everyone talking at once.

'How's that, then?'

'It's because of the updrafts.'

'What the hell are you on about? Bloody updrafts!'

'The rock causes these massive updrafts, what with the wind and everything. And it throws the bombs off course. It's a well-known fact, I'm telling you.'

'It's a well-known fact that you talk a load of bollocks.'

There was always nonsense talk like that in the ship's mess decks. Someone would air an opinion on something they knew nothing about and suddenly it'd be around the ship as if it had come from the captain himself.

I liked Gibraltar. We went ashore and, of course, Charlie was proved right, just like he said he would be. There were indeed monkeys living on the Rock of Gibraltar. Someone told us the old myth that says if the monkeys ever leave, British reign over Gibraltar will end. We took folklore like that seriously back then. It was reassuring I suppose.

Our first big job in the Mediterranean came early in July, just a few days after the fall of France. We were ordered to attack the French battle fleet tied up in the harbour at Oran, in Algeria. Britain couldn't afford to have those ships escape because it was a certainty that the newly installed pro-German Vichy French government would hand them over to the German Navy for use against us. Oran was only about 250 miles away on the North African coast, so we steamed urgently eastwards.

Oran had a harbour with a massive protective sea wall and the French ships were tucked away behind it. I was on the bridge watching through binoculars when they started getting up steam, ready to make a break. I could see the upper structures of the French ships quite clearly. *Valiant*'s 15-inch gun crews were called to action stations and they began to lob shells over the sea wall onto the trapped ships. The noise was stunning: violent booms followed by breath-taking screeches. Then smoke billowed from behind the sea wall.

I was amazed at what we were doing. One day the French were our allies, the next we were pumping 15-inch shells at their ships. We hit them terribly hard and I knew a lot of French sailors were dying, but all I felt was relief that there was no danger to *Valiant* in any of this.

This relief was swept aside almost immediately on our next job escorting a convoy carrying Hurricane fighters from Gibraltar to Malta. As we passed through the Straits of Pantelleria at night, our radar picked up ships approaching *Valiant*. Travelling at the speed they were, they had to be Italian motor torpedo boats. The Italians had a fine navy and those torpedo boats, their smallest, fastest craft, were potentially deadly. The call to action stations sounded through the ship and I rushed to my station inside the cramped compartment below the third 4.5 gun turret. As the Italian boats approached unseen in the darkness, the order was given.

'Fire!'

Inside the turret the warning bell sounded and a split second later our gun fired. Then I heard a massive explosion directly above me. As the gun next to us had turned onto its target, its inbuilt stopping mechanism had failed, causing it to swing right around and fire an armour piercing shell directly into our turret. There was utter chaos. Our turret filled with dense, choking smoke, and one chap tumbled off the pedestal above me. Another sailor was blasted backwards into our space below the gun, right at my feet. One of his arms was half blown away. Blood spurted from a gruesome, gaping hole in his side. Strangely, he didn't make a sound, but the rest of us were screaming. The urge to get out through the hatch behind us and abandon our post was overpowering, but just as pandemonium threatened, our petty officer 'Bugs' Roman saved the day. Bugs was a man whose many years in the navy had taught him the value of discipline when hell starts breaking loose.

'Misfire, misfire!' he yelled. 'Stand! Nobody move!'

At that, our training took over. We stayed, but my goodness, we needed the steadying influence of our petty officer. If it hadn't been for his presence of mind our action stations would have become panic stations.

The wounded sailor died right before our eyes. It was ghastly. And then it dawned on me that this was poor Hicks of the ridiculous marmalade jam argument. He lay dead at my feet and I was sick with regret.

I was never the same again.

4

Convoys, chaos and carnage

Despite the dreadful accident, *Valiant* never slowed. She just kept steaming through the Straights of Pantelleria, heading for Malta. The apparent threat from the Italian torpedo boats didn't materialise. It seemed to me that Hicks had died for no reason at all.

Two slow, war-weary biplanes flew out to meet the convoy as we approached Malta. They were hopelessly outdated and outclassed Gloster Gladiators of the Royal Air Force, known to the people of Malta as *Faith* and *Hope*. Along with another Gladiator called *Charity*, which had been destroyed the previous year, they had become the last heroic lynchpin in the defence of Malta. Their pilots must have been cheered by the sight of our convoy, because they knew it was bringing new Hurricanes for them.

But *Valiant* didn't stop at Malta, sailing on to Alexandria instead. There, in January 1941, we joined Admiral Cunningham's C Force. We moored in Alexandria Harbour, right next to a warship of the French fleet that was being guarded by the British. The French sailors were still on board under a form of house arrest. Like our earlier attack on the French battle fleet at Oran, this was to prevent the ship from being handed over to the Germans by the Vichy French government. We'd sit out on *Valiant*'s deck and watch them, and they'd sit on their deck and watch us back. That was pretty strange. But it was good to be in Alexandria because it gave us a chance to rest up. An ordnance crew came aboard and got to work repairing the damage to our turret. Fear had begun to invade me in an insidious way, but I kept a lid on it as best I could.

Bloody hell, what's going to happen next?

Whenever we went ashore in Alexandria we headed straight to the Fleet Club, a Royal Navy establishment where the British crews anchored in Alexandria Harbour gathered to eat, drink, swap yarns and get into fights over trivial matters, like whose ship was bigger and better. It was terrific, the Fleet Club, noisy and boisterous with its big bar, billiard tables, and frantic Egyptian waiters serving cheap meals. My shipmates and I always ordered the same: steak, eggs and chips with well-done fried onions and a pint of beer, followed by quite a few more pints. I used to love that. It got me in the frame of mind for having fun.

Some of the Alexandria locals travelled about in horse-drawn carts called gharries. One day a group of us at the Fleet Club got talking about those gharries in an idle, beer-fuelled kind of way.

'We need our own personal transport, that's what we need,' said 'Scouse' Parker, another sailor from *Valiant* who'd joined our regular drinking group.

'Yeah, our own personal transport.'

'A gharry would be perfect,' Parker said.

'How could we get one, do you think?' Freddie asked.

'We could steal one,' Johnny suggested.

'No, we'll *commandeer* one.'

'Even better.'

So we agreed to commandeer a gharry. Only a combination of beer and youth can make that seem like a good idea. Out we went into the crowded streets of Alexandria and pretty soon we saw a gharry that took our fancy.

'Does anyone know how to drive a gharry?' I asked. I had driven a horse-drawn laundry van, but didn't think that counted for much.

'I do,' said Parker.

'Then we appoint you our official gharry driver,' I said.

'I accept.'

It was easier than I thought. We simply approached the gharry, hoisted out the driver and poured ourselves in. The poor driver protested loudly but the beer made us indifferent. Besides, none of us understood Arabic.

'What's he saying?'

'Haven't got a clue.'

Parker grabbed hold of the reins with great flair and off we galloped. It was an interesting drive, but only for about five seconds. After that it seemed more dangerous than being on a battleship. Parker didn't have the faintest idea what he was doing.

'I thought you said you could drive a gharry!' I yelled from the back.

'I didn't say I could drive this one.'

'Oh.'

'Tell the bloody horse to stop!'

'What good's that going to do?' Parker said, heaving back on the reins. 'He doesn't understand English.'

'Silly me.'

With the horse out of control, the gharry swerved all

over the narrow street, people yelling at us and leaping out of the way. Pretty soon Parker realised he was a hopeless gharry driver and abandoned any further attempts at controlling the horse. He let go of the reins and thankfully the animal stopped. A little shaken, but laughing uncontrollably, we abandoned the gharry and slipped unsteadily into the crowd.

At other times I would set off around Alexandria by myself. I really enjoyed that colourful place, with its chaotic back alleys and bazaars, all crammed with pokey shops and open-air stalls. It was dirty, noisy and packed with jostling, yelling people. The air was sharp with spices and the pungent smells of strange food cooking. I thought it was wonderful in an exotic, slightly mysterious way.

The traders got excited whenever they saw British sailors approaching. They pushed and poked us, holding their wares up in front of our faces, demanding we spend our money. It was possible to buy just about anything in the back alleys and bazaars of Alexandria. It was even possible to buy a woman. One of my mates, Peter Rimmer, was always on the lookout for 'blue' photographs. By today's standards I suppose they were tame, but back then they were definitely considered illicit. Peter had quite a collection, which he guarded jealously.

After our runs ashore we'd go back to the ship and confront reality again. I began to dread the telltale signs that our force was getting ready for sea again. We'd see 'flashing up': smoke belching from the funnels of ships in the harbour and pennants going up all over the place.

Oh, oh. Here we go again. Where is it this time?

We'd steam out of Alexandria Harbour and maybe a couple of hours later they'd tell us where we were going. It was usually to Malta, escorting yet another convoy. We were invariably shadowed by the Luftwaffe's long-range Condor reconnaissance aircraft, so were always on high-alert. We accompanied the aircraft carrier HMS *Illustrious* on a number of those Malta convoys. She had Faircy Fulmar and Swordfish aircraft of the Fleet Air Arm aboard, which at least gave us some air cover. They were courageous blokes who flew in those Swordfish. They had open cockpits and were made of wood, fabric and bracing wire, so the crews were often exposed to the fury of bad weather. 'String bags', we used to call them. They flew very slowly and were sitting ducks.

As these convoys continued through February and March, I stood my watch as usual on *Valiant*'s bridge. Often a young blond midshipman would be up there with us. He had joined the ship in Alexandria in January. He was an ADO, an Air Defence Officer, and his job was to coordinate the searchlights and lookouts scanning the skies for aircraft. He was a little older than me and his name was Prince Philip of Greece. Sometimes he would chat to us, but otherwise kept to himself. He was just another crewman as far as we were concerned, no one special at all.

We often stopped in Malta, and I hated that. The Italians regularly bombed Valetta Harbour, although it was a little safer because of the protection offered by the RAF Hurricanes we had escorted across from Gibraltar. The Italians bombed us from high altitude, and not all that accurately, but when the Germans came into the Mediterranean they brought their dreaded Stuka dive-bombers with them. They'd use them on us whether we were at sea or holed up in the harbour at Malta. We'd see them high up, then they'd roll over into a near-vertical dive with their characteristic high-pitched scream. It was terrifying, that sound. Sometimes the RAF Hurricanes would streak over to take on the Stukas in snarling dogfights. I was frightened most of the time on those convoys, and judging by the frantic rush to the heads after the Stukas departed, I wasn't the only one. Stukas must be the best laxative ever developed. It was like that all the way to Malta, and all the way back again. I didn't think there could be anything more terrifying than a Stuka attack.

Our work in the Mediterranean often involved support for the British Army along the North Africa coast, bombarding enemy positions with our 15-inch guns. Once we attacked a position near Bardiyah, just east of Tobruk, firing into the big sandy cliffs at the water's edge. Then, out of nowhere the cliffs started firing back. The culprit was a white fort on top of the escarpment.

'The bloody cheek,' fumed our gunnery officer. 'We can't have that. Demolish that thing immediately!'

On his command, our gunners swung all eight of *Valiant*'s 15-inch guns to the same side of the ship and fired them simultaneously in a vicious broadside. There was a tremendous blast as the shells shrieked off toward the coast, leaving a great cloud of brown cordite smoke to drift down the length of the ship. The gunners' range-finding was immaculate: the shells all hit the cliff in a neat line directly beneath the fort, which, after a pause, slid to the beach below and disintegrated. I tried not to think of the people in that fort, but it wasn't possible.

They've got mothers and fathers, sisters and brothers, just like me. They're ordinary people, and we've just killed the whole bloody lot of them. But it was war and we couldn't change what was going on, so I did my best to switch off. But burying those sorts of feelings takes its toll.

In between jobs like the fort at Bardiyah, we'd steam back to Alexandria and lie up in the harbour to resume our pastime of eyeballing the French sailors. Being back in harbour was a mixed blessing for me. It was much less dangerous, but there was a lot more time to think. And as 1941 wore on it became difficult not to dwell on the bad news coming from the home front. Britain was still under siege. London, Coventry, Manchester and my home city of Liverpool were all being bombed by the Luftwaffe.

Will I still have a home to go to when all this is over?

And there was a buzz around the mess decks that disturbed me greatly.

'Canada, that's where we'll be off to if things don't start looking up,' I heard a sailor say.

'Canada? Why Canada?'

'In case we lose the war.'

'Who says we're going to lose the war?' another bloke protested. 'Like hell we'll lose the bloody war!'

'If it looks like we're going to lose, they'll withdraw *Valiant* and all the other big ships to Canada. We'll be the Free English, in exile over in Canada. You know, just like the Free French in exile now in Britain.'

That got the usual mess deck response.

'Bullshit!'

'You'll see. We'll all end up being Canadians.'

It was dreadfully depressing to hear talk like that. Defeat was in the air. I became morose and fearful, besieged by lonely, chilling thoughts about the very real possibility of dying, piled on top of the usual nightmares about Stukas screaming overhead.

We never got sent to Canada, but in the last week of March, the Royal Navy sent *Valiant* and the other ships of our force to intercept an Italian fleet assembling in the eastern Mediterranean. Acting on an air reconnaissance report from their German allies, the Italian ships had sailed from ports in Italy to attack a large British convoy. Our job, together with the aircraft carrier HMS *Formidable*, HMS *Warspite* and Admiral Cunningham's flagship HMS *Barham*, was to protect the convoy.

During the night of 29 March, the tannoy in *Valiant* clicked on, hissed and crackled like it always did, and the captain told us that we were going to be engaging in a naval battle with ships of the Italian fleet. Just like that. A matter of fact.

A naval battle? That can't be right. I'm just a Liverpool lad, people like me don't take part in naval battles!

A bugle trumpeted over the tannoy, sounding the call to raise the battle flag, the only time I heard that rare call on a warship. It was followed by the more familiar bugle call to action stations, so I rushed to my gun turret.

Valiant was the only ship in our force with radar, one of the original radar systems used at sea during the war. It had a range of about 100 miles, pretty good for those days, but as it turned out we didn't need any such range on the night of the 29th. Just after 10 o'clock the radar detected three Italian cruisers, *Pola*, *Fiume* and *Zara*, a mere six miles away. They were steaming with their guns pointing fore and aft, oblivious to the ships of our force approaching. The weather was quite good that night, so to this day I've never been able to fathom why their lookouts didn't see us.

Still undetected, we steered onto a parallel course within 4000 yards of them, and swung our 15-inch and 4.5 guns broadside to the Italians. *Warspite* did the same. On *Valiant*'s bridge, Prince Philip was coordinating our searchlights. He caught the enemy ships in a blinding, blue-white illumination, and we were given the order to fire. Those poor Italians didn't stand a chance. Our armour-piercing shells pummelled them and caused devastating damage. The three cruisers sank within a few minutes. They didn't even have time to fire a single shot back at us. Another two Italian destroyers were also lost in a different engagement in the same battle. Some 2400 Italian sailors lost their lives.

It was over in no time at all and I was glad to get out of that without being fired on. The thought of being sunk filled me with horror. But it was another job done, so we turned for Alexandria, all the while expecting to be attacked from the air. Nothing happened, so we got away with it nicely.

And that was the Battle of Matapan. As an ordinary seaman on a battleship, it's possible to take part in a naval engagement without even realising that it might be historically significant. The ship is so big and complex, with so many people doing hundreds of different jobs, that no one is ever told all the details that make up the big picture. An ordinary seaman doesn't know why it's happening, or how a situation has come about. He's just told the bare facts. He's a very small player in what is actually a deadly game of chess played with opposing ships on a huge area of sea, with the opponents mostly out of sight of one another.

Back in harbour I kept thinking about those Italian ships going to the bottom, packed with sailors like me. The tension was building in me terribly. But I couldn't dwell on it because the Germans suddenly invaded Greece and Crete, so they sent us to Crete during May.

Dear Lord, here we go again.

We went into Suda Bay, the harbour on Crete, and once again we were sitting ducks. The RAF never seemed to cover us, and the Germans were only about 90 miles away with their aircraft and paratroopers. Suda was a volcanic place where the water was the clearest I'd ever seen. I could see the bottom of the harbour below the ship's bilges when I looked over *Valiant*'s deck railing.

Why do they keep sending us into places like this? They're really pushing our luck.

The Germans bombed us nearly every day and night while we were in the harbour. We were constantly called to action stations. It seemed the Luftwaffe had started a shuttle service. They came over from Greece, dropped their bombs, went back to Greece, refilled their bomb bays and came out to attack us again.

One day in Suda Bay, a snarling swarm of Stuka dive-bombers singled *Valiant* out for some close attention. We rushed again to action stations, elevated our 4.5 guns and commenced firing. It was bedlam closed up inside our turret. My head was reeling from the din of the gun firing and the clatter of empty shells spilling onto the deck. The attack lasted for about 15 minutes before we were given the order to cease firing. We emerged from our turret to find the quarterdeck in chaos. Two bombs had exploded there but, by some miracle, no one was killed. A few of the crew aft on the upper deck were wounded, though. I knew one of the blokes who got hurt, Tubby Herks, a big round-faced Scot. He was badly shaken up and other sailors in that part of the ship were trying to sort out the smoking wreckage. They looked dazed and ashen. Holed up in our turret, we hadn't even felt the bombs explode.

Although the damage to the ship was slight, this attack was enough to convince the Royal Navy that we shouldn't be in places like Suda Bay where the Luftwaffe could bomb us at will. So we made some hasty repairs and steamed back to Alexandria. As soon as we got ashore we set course for the Fleet Club and had a few settling drinks.

Conversation in the Fleet Club often got around to the sailors who suddenly vanished from the ship after reporting sick. I don't know what became of them, whether they were sent to jobs ashore in Alexandria or got shipped back to England. But they were removed from the ship very quickly, because uncontrollable fear in one person can spread to others.

'Where's so-and-so?' someone might ask, mentioning a sailor we all knew.

'He reported sick.'

'Bomb happy,' someone else would say. That explained everything.

'Poor bastard.'

No one ever blamed those men, or thought any less of them. We were all struggling in silence with our own anxieties. I had begun to notice the strain on the faces of the other young seamen around me. They looked older. I wondered if I looked like that. I was determined to keep going because I didn't want to let my mates down, and I knew they didn't want to let me down. That's what being part of a ship's crew is all about, a sense of mutual obligation. But we were all riding an emotional roller coaster.

The lows were sometimes horrific. When we weren't at the Fleet Club, escorting convoys or doing other jobs at sea, we'd spend long periods on the ship as she rode at her mooring in Alexandria Harbour. This meant we were available to go aboard any battle-damaged ships to help clear up. Once I was assigned to a working party when one of our cruisers struggled into harbour after taking a direct hit during an air raid. A bomb had crashed through the steel deck of the bridge, and exploded in the mess deck far below. The carnage was unspeakable. There were bits of bodies scattered everywhere and the stench was nauseating. It was the smell of death and the memory of it lives on for a lifetime.

None of us wanted to be part of it, but we were ordered to get the job done and not talk about what we'd seen. Every single member of that working party was shaken to the core. It was soul-destroying, heart-wrenching and desperately sad. These days, I dare say the men of such a working party would receive counselling. But there was nothing like that then, nobody at all for us to talk to. That was how it was, and not just for people in uniform. Civilians were 'cleaning up' after their neighbours' houses had been destroyed in air raids, their own families were being bombed and killed as well, at home in England, here in Africa, wherever the battles were being fought. Like the sea, bombs don't make any distinctions.

Fortunately, there was also plenty to keep us laughing. On *Valiant*, many of the lighter moments were provided by a dishevelled Canadian sailor called Banjo Bailey, a misfit, hostilities-only volunteer from Saskatchewan. Whether he had been in catering as a civilian I'm not sure, but he worked below decks in the galleys. No amount of navy discipline seemed to convince Banjo to tidy himself up. His hat was never straight and he always looked unshaven. Once, when I was on watch, Banjo presented himself on the bridge with a side of meat slung over his shoulder. Everyone looked at him in astonishment.

'What's that then, Bailey?' an officer enquired.

'It's a side of meat, sir.' He spoke with a slow drawl.

'I can see that, man. But why in God's name have you brought it up here?'

'I was just told to take it to the bridge, sir.'

A pause while the officer worked it out. 'I think you'll find you were ordered to take it to the *fridge*, Bailey.'

'Aye aye, sir,' Banjo said. He about-faced and left the bridge, as confused as everyone else.

Without fail, we all got our rum issue every morning at 11 o'clock. It was beautiful rum, too, good stuff with a lovely dark, reddish colour. One morning, while we were escorting a convoy to Malta, we were at action stations when 'Up spirits!' came over the tannoy. But because we were all closed up in the turret, no one in our gun crew could leave their post to collect the rum issue. So Banjo was sent below to get it for us. He returned empty-handed.

'Where's the rum, Banjo?'

'Couldn't find any,' he drawled.

'There must be a rum issue down there somewhere.'

'I didn't see any.' He seemed perplexed, as always.

'Well, what was down there, then?'

'Nothing.'

'Nothing? What about on the mess table?'

'Oh,' Banjo said, his memory jogged. 'There was this thing, a big container.'

'And ...' we chorused helpfully. We were desperate for our rum ration. It was always in that container.

'I looked in it but it was only cold tea, so I chucked it away.' Banjo was lucky to escape alive.

Apart from lifting the spirits and keeping us warm, rum was also valuable currency. The rum was for drinking there and then, according to the navy. But by building up a supply, blokes could use it for barter. Get someone to cut their hair, do their washing, things like that. I always drank my rum straight away, though. Like I said, it was good stuff. And it always made me incredibly hungry. Once I'd downed my rum I could eat my way through a stack of the corned beef sandwiches that were always available on board. Even when we were at action stations the galley crew would bring us corned beef sandwiches. The best sandwiches ever, they were.

Our convoy duties dragged on through 1941, with no

indication that we'd be going home any time soon. About the only highlight was when I turned 20 in October.

Then, in the last week of November we sailed from Alexandria in the company of our sister battleships HMS *Queen Elizabeth* and HMS *Barham* as well as eight destroyers. We were to join up with a bigger Allied fleet and intercept two large Italian convoys believed to be making for Benghazi in Libya. On the afternoon of 25 November our group was patrolling south of Crete when, without any warning, *Barham* was hit by three torpedoes fired from a German U-boat that had skilfully penetrated our line of defending cruisers. Surely fate was at work for me here. That submarine commander could easily have fired at *Valiant*, with me closed up at action stations below my 4.5 turret, but instead he selected *Barham* through his periscope.

When the torpedoes hit her, *Barham* rolled on her side almost immediately. We heard a dull rumble, then a massive explosion as her store of ammunition blew up. Less than three minutes later she had completely disappeared, dragging more than 850 men with her to the bottom of the Mediterranean. There is a famous piece of film showing *Barham* rolling over with some of her desperate crew massing on her upturned side. I don't know who shot the film, or what ship he was on when he captured *Barham*'s last moments, but it is spellbinding and chilling. It could have been me and my shipmates clinging to *Valiant*'s hull, with just seconds to live before she blew up. Amazingly, about 450 crewmen survived and were rescued.

Immediately after firing her torpedoes, the U-boat erupted from the water right in front of *Valiant*. This happened sometimes when a submarine, cruising just beneath the surface, relieved itself of the weight of its torpedoes. The lookouts on our bridge watched incredulously as the sub's conning tower passed right down the side of us. She was so close that we couldn't depress our guns far enough to fire at her. *Valiant* immediately began to turn around with the intention of ramming the U-boat on the surface, but our turning arc was huge and by the time we'd come around, the enemy vessel had managed to crash dive. We passed harmlessly over the top of it.

After that job we went back to the relative safety of Alexandria harbour where, early in December, I was promoted to able seaman. *Maybe I'll be sent home for Christmas with my family.* No such luck, though. The war had other ideas. Early on a calm Mediterranean night, I was in our mess when the quiet of the evening was punctuated by a bugle call that a sailor never wants to hear.

'Clear lower deck! Clear lower deck!' Something was seriously wrong. No one waited for an explanation. We just rushed to the upper deck.

'The enemy has attacked our ship here in the harbour,' the captain told us in his usual matter of fact way.

In harbour, we always had Royal Marine sentries on board, patrolling the decks. The sentry on our bow had spied figures clinging to *Valiant*'s mooring buoy in the darkness and a small boat had been dispatched to investigate. The figures turned out to be Italian navy frogmen. They were captured and brought aboard the ship where, under questioning, they admitted to attaching limpet mines to *Valiant*'s hull.

'These gentlemen seem reluctant to tell us where exactly

on the hull these mines are located,' the captain said. 'So to encourage them to do so we are going to put them down in the lower deck.'

Shortly after the Italians had been taken below, muffled explosions came from deep in the ship. No one was hurt but, in an instant, our great battleship was disabled. She was down at the bow. This courageous attack by the Italians shocked us all, especially because *Valiant*'s sister ship *Queen Elizabeth*, moored near us, had suffered a similar attack and was already listing badly to starboard. Even in harbour, we realised, there was no escape from war.

With *Valiant* disabled, a group of my shipmates and I were told to report to the master-at-arms' office. We were going to be drafted away from the ship.

Perhaps this is it. Maybe we're going home.

I began to cheer up at the prospect, as I hadn't been home since November 1939, but I was handed a written draft chit posting me to shore duties at Port Said in Egypt, at the entrance to the Suez Canal. Johnny, Charlie, Davey and Peter were all posted with me but Freddie had orders to remain on *Valiant*. Peter packed his collection of dubious photographs in his duffle bag.

'We'll be a bit safer in Port Said.'

'Maybe,' Johnny said doubtfully. 'But it might be a hell of a lot more dangerous.'

So in January 1942 we reported to Navy House, a big building overlooking the jetty at Port Said. This would be our accommodation. I was put on general shore duties, which meant patrolling the quayside on foot, protecting the British military installations there.

'Protecting them from what?' I asked.

'Egyptians in boats,' I was told.

'What do I do if I see Egyptians in boats?'

'Shoot them.' I must have looked alarmed. 'Don't kill them, just scare them off. Don't let anyone approach the quay.'

Well, this was certainly different from being aboard a battleship. All that training in seamanship and here I was, a sentry with a rifle and orders to shoot at Egyptians approaching in boats. It wasn't terribly exciting, but that suited me fine. We did have a few air raids, and I had to make a dash for cover occasionally, but they didn't come to much. The only Allied aircraft we saw were RAF Wellington bombers fitted with huge metal rings that completely surrounded them. The rings created a magnetic field that exploded enemy mines, so the Wellingtons would fly low past the quay on their way to make the Canal safer for Allied shipping.

Each of the navy sentries patrolling the quay was assigned an interpreter. Mine was a Greek civilian called Minoli Kambouris who spoke excellent English and perfect Arabic. On my instructions, he'd call out to any small boats that approached, warning them I'd shoot if they didn't bugger off. Minoli was a lovely man. He taught me snippets of Greek and Arabic, and from time to time he'd take me to his home in Port Said to spend time with his family. They were a very kind, welcoming lot. I enjoyed doing that, meeting new people and going into a family home. It was a break from the boredom.

After I'd been on sentry duty for a couple of months,

Johnny Hennessey and I were assigned as an armed escort taking some British soldiers to an internment camp at Ismailiya, which is on the Canal about halfway between Port Said and Suez, near the Bitter Lakes. They had committed various crimes and were to serve their sentences at that dreadful place. Johnny and I presented our papers to the sentry at the camp gate but as soon as we'd handed the soldiers over, they were set upon by a brutal bunch of military policemen. I was shocked. They'd barely set foot in the camp and already they were being mercilessly kicked and punched.

'You can't treat those blokes like that!' I protested.

'On your way, sailor,' one of the MPs snarled. 'It's none of your bloody business. Go on, piss off.'

By this time I'd just about had enough of all things military. I left feeling disturbed, churning inside. Utterly fed up, I went back to patrolling the quay with Minoli. At the end of June I got another draft chit. This time, together with Johnny, Peter and Davey, I was detailed to escort a contingent of Italian prisoners-of-war to Durban in South Africa. Our hopes soared.

'This is more like it,' Davey said.

'Durban's a long way from the hot spots.'

'Better than all the bullshit at Navy House.'

We sailed to Durban with the Italian prisoners on a Polish passenger ship, going via the Suez Canal to Port Suez, then through the Red Sea for a brief stop in baking-hot Aden. Then we sailed into the Indian Ocean, calling in at Mombassa, and finally down the east coast of Africa. The Italian prisoners gave us no trouble at all and we arrived in Durban around the middle of August.

Then, with Johnny, Peter and Davey, I was sent to a military staging camp at Pietermaritzburg, in the hills to the west of Durban. It was absolutely wonderful there. The war hadn't touched the area at all, so it felt like peacetime. The air was beautifully cool and fresh and there was plenty of food. It was heaven, even though we were sleeping in tents. It was just nice to feel the peace soaking into me, damping down my ragged nerves. Every morning the local farmers left gallons of fresh milk outside our tents, the sweetest milk I'd ever tasted.

We'd been in that invigorating camp for a couple of weeks when more draft chits came. I couldn't believe it. We were being drafted back to England! The relief was almost overwhelming.

It's over. I'm actually going home! You're all right now, Jim.

It was the most fantastic feeling, the best news I'd had since I was drafted to *Valiant* back in 1939. My mates and I returned to the port at Durban in high spirits. We would be embarking on a ship berthed some distance away from the main quays. It was a passenger liner. I stared at it.

'That looks bloody familiar, that ship,' I told the others. 'It's a Cunard ship.' Anyone who'd grown up in Liverpool would recognise those distinctive lines.

We walked along to look at the ship that was going to take us home. As I got closer I was stunned to see *Laconia* on the bow, still visible beneath its coarse coat of wartime grey.

'Well, bloody hell!'

'What's up?'

'I know this ship,' I said. 'My father was the first-class steward.'

Here was the most amazing omen, I figured. Someone was guiding me, surely. I was going home on my father's last ship, a ship I'd been aboard and loved as a boy. She looked neglected, but beneath her sea stains and shabby paint I could see it was the same wonderful *Laconia*.

'This is meant to be,' I told the others. I was totally convinced of it. It was 28 August 1942, and I was going home.

5

Terror in the night

Along with Lieutenant Tillie, the officer in charge of our draft, we joined a small Royal Navy contingent on *Laconia*. The once spic-and-span Cunard lady wasn't quite the ship I remembered. The war had changed her like it had changed all of us. She appeared tired, overworked, unkempt and utterly functional. Gone were the garden lounges, potted palms and smoking lounges, replaced by the austere fittings of war. But underneath her ugly grey paint, she was the same ship I'd been on with my father. I'd forgotten much about her, so, along with my mates, I spent the first few hours aboard having a good look around.

'I just saw a woman,' Johnny reported in astonishment.

'A woman! Bollocks, you've been at sea too bloody long.'

'She was no ordinary woman, either. She was a nurse.'

'We've joined a pleasure cruise by mistake,' I suggested.

'And there are kids here as well,' Peter said. 'Mothers with babies and all.'

'That's something different.'

Our navy contingent had been tossed into the sort of melting pot of humanity that only a war can conjure up. For a start there was *Laconia*'s crew. Then there were 1800 Italian prisoners-of-war and their Polish guards, a group of women and children from Palestine, some nursing sisters, and hundreds of army and air force personnel fresh from duty in Malta and the Middle East. There were 2700 people on board, all sailing for England. In peacetime *Laconia* only ever carried 2000 passengers at most, so it was going to be a very crowded voyage.

We were allocated quarters in the stern, on one of the lower decks, and assigned our on-board jobs. Unlike the army and air force types, who were taking passage home, we had to work. In the navy there's no such thing as a free ride.

'If we've joined a pleasure cruise,' Peter grumbled, 'the pleasure is going to be everyone else's.'

'Bloody typical, that is,' we moaned.

Lieutenant Tillie assigned Johnny, Peter and I to augment one of the DEMS gun crews. DEMS stood for Defence Equipment Merchant Ships, and *Laconia*'s gun crew was responsible for manning the big six-inch gun bolted to the deck on the stern. We were pretty fed up with guns by then, but they were our orders and that was that.

After we'd settled ourselves in, I got to thinking about Fred Eyres, who had been *Laconia*'s pantry-man when I was a lad. I asked one of the crew if he was on board.

'You mean Fred the pantry-man?'

'That'd be him,' I said.

'Why do you want to see the pantry-man?'

'He was a neighbour of mine in Liverpool.'

'I'll tell him you're here.'

Fred soon appeared on deck and cast a puzzled eye over our group of sailors.

'Do you remember me, Fred?' I asked. He looked me up and down and eventually smiled.

'You're Benjamin's boy, aren't you?'

'That's right. It's Jim.'

'Well I'll be . . . young Jim McLoughlin.'

We shook hands warmly. I was pleased to be in the company of someone who knew my family. He was in his 50s by then, an old man to me, but he seemed glad to see me. I told him about my time serving on *Valiant*, and we chatted about the war and going home. Then he said: 'You can always come down to my station and have a meal, you know.'

'I'd like that,' I said.

'You'll eat better with the pantry-man than anywhere else on this ship.'

This was no idle promise. Eating on a ship's mess deck was always a mad scramble, the food usually best forgotten. But the pantry-man, well, he had the food stores at his fingertips. So here was something to look forward to, a decent meal with someone who knew where I came from, someone who'd worked with my father on this very ship.

'I'll come and see you when I've got some free time,' I promised.

'Two decks below, forward on the starboard side.'

Laconia slipped out of Durban at the end of August, heading for Cape Town where she tied up for two days and we were given some shore leave. After our wonderful stay in the hills behind Durban, I had grown fond of life in South Africa. It seemed a place of plenty to me, untainted by war, and especially beautiful with its stunning landmark of Table Mountain forever at its back.

Laconia sailed from Cape Town on Friday 4 September

and commenced its voyage north-west into the Atlantic. As the first few hours passed, I was filled with expectations of home. Then the old anxieties surfaced again, because we were not part of a convoy. *Laconia* was sailing alone in the Atlantic, which I knew was a dangerous place indeed. To make matters worse, the ship was belching a huge black stain of smoke from her funnel.

'The U-boats'll see that smoke before we even appear on the horizon,' someone said. 'We may as well broadcast our exact position.'

'She's zigzagging, though.'

'What, and that's supposed to shake off a U-boat?'

Bloody hell. Here we go again.

The passengers, it seemed, were blissfully ignorant of the danger, and it was probably just as well. We mentioned it to various members of *Laconia*'s crew, but they just shrugged.

'Can't do anything about it,' they said. 'She just smokes like that all the time. She's an old ship. What do you expect us to do, stop and drop anchor?'

As if the thick black pall wasn't enough of a giveaway, our gun crew had to conduct practice drills every day which meant blazing away at an imaginary target in the water. Our six-inch gun fired shell after shell into the sea, sending up great plumes of white water.

'Here we are!' the gun proclaimed. And in a very loud voice at that.

The familiar tight knot returned to my stomach, but I settled into the shipboard routine well enough. The days grew hot as we steamed north-west, and the nights passed without much happening. Our contingent didn't mix with the other passengers at all. Because the ship was so crowded, we mainly just stayed in our stern quarters. Occasionally we'd chat to the crew or watch groups of Italian prisoners getting fresh air and exercise with their Polish guards.

On the night of Saturday 12 September we were far out into the Atlantic, approximately north-east of Ascension Island and approaching the equator. It was a clear night. I hadn't yet had my meal with Fred, so I decided to see him that evening. I was very hungry because I hadn't eaten since lunchtime and back then I was a big lad, about 13 or 14 stone. I was looking forward to that meal, I really was. I didn't tell my mates where I was going.

Remembering Fred's directions, I went down a wooden staircase, past a lot of troops sitting around smoking and playing cards without a care in the world. I had just reached the bottom of a second staircase when there was a brain-numbing explosion as a torpedo struck the ship.

The noise was crushing. I felt like I'd been punched in the head by a powerful fist of sound. It turned my head to putty. Then it wrapped around me, lifted me off my feet and hurled me backwards into a steel bulkhead, leaving me gasping and crumpled on the deck. The lights went out and there was an eerie silence that lasted for perhaps a few seconds. Then pandemonium erupted. People were screaming and crying out. I was on my hands and knees, trying to get up, but there was a rush of bodies all around me. Everyone was pushing and shoving and trampling and cursing in the blackness, trying to reach the staircase I'd just come down. I had to get back up that staircase.

I got to my feet and even though I was dazed and shocked,

I could tell that the deck was sloping to starboard, mere seconds after the torpedo had hit. She was going down already. I made for the staircase.

But then came another huge, rumbling explosion, this time further along the ship toward the bow. *Laconia* shuddered beneath my feet. A new wave of terror swelled and rushed through the blackness. The confined space of the stairwell was awash with people screaming for their lives, calling out names, swearing. It was chilling.

I got up that first staircase very quickly and made for the second. Even in the darkness I knew where it would be. But when I arrived, swept along by the desperate, seething humanity around me, the staircase had gone. My eyes had adjusted to the darkness and I could make out vague shapes and people around me, looking up at a dim square where the staircase had been. I started feeling around for the Jacob's ladder that I'd seen when I first came aboard.

On many ships, there was often a Jacob's ladder shackled to the rim of the stairwell and hanging behind the permanent stairs, just simple wooden rungs between two pieces of wire. They weren't easy things to climb at the best of times because the wires tended to twist around on themselves. But in the darkness and surrounded by jostling, screaming people, it would be doubly difficult. It had to be climbed from the side, with one of the wires between the legs. That way it stayed straight.

I was fit and strong and knew I could climb it. The alternative was being trapped below. I groped frantically in front of me and found it within seconds. Other people were swarming around, grappling with the awkward ladder, trying to work out how to climb it. I just went straight up, like a monkey on a vine. It was no time for saying: 'No, please, after you.' People started following me up, clutching at my legs as I went, but some of them fell back into the darkness below, all the time screaming and yelling. It was hard to pull myself clear of all the clawing hands.

I emerged from the stairwell on the starboard side of the ship, the low side, and it was absolute bloody mayhem. Big unrestrained objects were sliding and tumbling down the deck. Some of them were screaming people. Human shapes were stumbling about as if they were walking around the side of a steep hill, because the deck was already at a pretty sharp angle. The bow was down as well, so I struggled to stay upright. People were crawling to get up higher. Panic-stricken voices were yelling into the night. There were no deck lights at all so it was a maelstrom of noise and frantic shapes rushing and stumbling.

Amid all the chaos I noticed strange, sharp little explosions that didn't belong on a ship, like fireworks going off. It was small arms fire ricocheting off *Laconia*'s superstructure. The Italian prisoners had found their way onto the deck and their Polish guards were trying to keep them under control. It was a totally unexpected danger. I had to get somewhere safer, if there was such a place.

I started to think a bit more clearly, and focussed on mustering at my station. That says plenty about my training, I think. My ship was sinking, but I didn't think of getting to a lifeboat. Instead, I groped toward the stern and eventually got to our six-inch gun. It was a little quieter back there, and Johnny and Peter had already arrived. We agreed it was pointless manning the gun. There was nothing to fire at. The U-boat that had blasted our ship would be long gone. The stern was rising as *Laconia* went down further at the bow. There was absolutely nothing we could do.

'Bugger the gun,' Peter said. 'I'm going back to get me photographs.'

'Your what?'

'Me dirty photographs. I can't just leave 'em, I'm going back below.' Johnny and I looked at him in total disbelief as he started to move off.

'You're bloody mad, come here!' I yelled, grabbing him. But he shook me off as he headed below to find his photographs. I couldn't believe it. I was convinced he was going off to a watery grave. It was by far the craziest thing I've ever seen anyone do.

Johnny and I knew the lifeboats would be chaotic and that we'd have a better chance if we just went over the high side. That was the port side. In our training they had always said to us: 'Never go over the low side when a ship's going down. Always go over the high side. That way, if she rolls over, you won't be trapped underneath.' That seemed like wise advice, so we set off along the deck on the high side. There were people flying around everywhere in the darkness. The turmoil was getting worse as everyone realised she was sinking steadily. Then, in the blink of an eye, Johnny disappeared. One moment he was there beside me, the next he had vanished.

I looked over the port-side railing at the water a long, long way down. The stern was incredibly high. Terror gripped me in a deep, ice-cold dread.

There's no bloody way I'm going down there.

In a split second I decided to ignore the navy's good advice, and slid down the sloping deck to the starboard side where the water was much closer. I found a rope trailing over the side. Someone had obviously gone over before me. That was good enough for me. I took off my boots and lowered myself hand over hand into the sea. I had to get as far away as possible from the doomed ship because as soon as she went down, the boilers would explode and the concussion would spread through the water like a battering ram. It could kill me. And when she sank there would be a massive circular eddy of water that would suck everything down with it. I swam for my life.

Oddly, I've never been able to remember whether the water was warm or cold when I first got into it. It simply didn't register. I could taste oil and there was debris knocking into me, but I kept swimming because I didn't have a lot of time. There were people flaying about, lunging at one another, desperately trying to hold on to anything and anyone. I didn't want frantic hands grabbing on to me and dragging me under, so I kept swimming strongly away from the ship. Fairly soon I came to a lifeboat. It was crowded, but I hauled myself in anyway. I was shocked to find myself knee-deep in water. Someone had forgotten to put the drainage bungs in before it was launched. The people in the boat weren't saying or doing anything while the water poured in. It was useless.

No bloody future in this. She'll go to the bottom before Laconia.

I got back into the water and looked over at *Laconia*. She was still too close for comfort, and her massive propellers were visible as her stern heaved further out of the water. They were turning slowly but the ship was strangely quiet. All the noise and commotion was coming from the water around her as people grappled with their own unthinkable situation. I turned and swam further away from the ship and finally came across a raft. When I first went on board *Laconia* in Durban, I'd noticed a number of wooden rafts lashed to the deck, obviously for just this kind of catastrophe. They weren't very big, just a few square feet really, nothing more. I joined a lot of other people clinging to loops of rope along each side of the raft. Everyone was covered in oil. Lieutenant Tillie was near me. He seemed to be badly injured.

Eventually I lost my grip and the raft drifted out of reach. I hadn't eaten anything since lunchtime, so the strength was draining from my arms. A short time later I came across another raft that was much less crowded, so I hung on to that and watched *Laconia* go down. It was terrifying and dreadfully painful to see such a wonderful ship in her death throes. She had been like a figurehead to me, a great source of pride during the carefree days of my boyhood in Liverpool. I was so mesmerised that I forgot my own predicament. I couldn't draw my eyes away because there is a terrible, grim fascination about a sinking ship. The need to watch it is inexplicably compelling.

Laconia's stern rose higher and her bow slid into the Atlantic at a steep angle, still listing heavily to starboard, the sea swallowing her emergency lights one by one. Then suddenly she heaved up almost to the vertical, before continuing her shocking plunge. I dragged myself onto the wooden raft to protect myself from the imminent explosion, leaving just my legs exposed in the water. As she dived, the boiling cacophony of hissing bubbles and groaning metal was incredible. There was a deep, evil guttural rumbling, then, when she had vanished, a huge booming blast as the boilers exploded below the surface. I felt the concussion through the timber of the raft as it swept by my legs like an invisible wave under the water.

It was weird. One moment the massive bulk of *Laconia* floundered mortally wounded beside us in the water and then, within seconds, there was nothing except debris and people floating about. Despite the shapes and ghostly reflections of hundreds of other people around me, I suddenly felt fearfully lost. The loneliness was devastating. I didn't have a bloody clue what to do next.

More and more people were scrambling around in the water, grabbing at the ropes and pulling on my legs as they jostled for a precious spot on the raft.

This is no good. You'll be safer by yourself.

I swam off again, desperately uncertain, and started bumping into dozens of dead bodies floating face down. I was swimming through a graveyard. It was a scene from a nightmare, except it was real and happening to me. Out of the ghostly darkness, another wooden raft drifted close to me, with just one bloke sitting on it. I called out to him and when he answered I thought I recognised the voice of my mate, Davey Jones.

'Is that you, Davey?'

'Who's that?'

'It's Mac!'

'Well, bloody hell.'

We couldn't believe our luck, meeting up with each other in all the dark chaos. I hauled myself onto the raft and sat next to him with my legs dangling in the water.

I had no idea what the time was. It had been just after eight o'clock when I went below to find Fred. The torpedoes hit *Laconia* just moments after that, so she might have gone down an hour later, but I wasn't sure. The night seemed suspended, as if holding its breath. Everything was dreamlike. I half expected to wake up and find myself safely back on the ship. Things were happening in slow motion and I began to feel a bit detached. It was the shock of it all, I suppose.

I was wet, numb with cold and fear, and utterly miserable. To this day I can still feel the complete numbness that spread through my body that night. But I also felt a rush of relief because someone reliable was with me and I didn't have to swim anymore. So there was a thin thread of hope.

Davey and I sat on that raft all night. The screaming and yelling around us subsided as the night dragged on, but we could still hear the occasional vague cry for help in the distance. We couldn't tell exactly where they were coming from. Once we thought we heard the throbbing of an engine close by. We couldn't work that out.

Dawn arrived like a curtain opening on a scene of total devastation. There were scores of bodies floating face down, bloated and grotesque, and there was debris everywhere. Boxes and tins drifted by. We were ravenously hungry and thirsty, so we started to pick some up in the hope of finding food. We weren't saying much, just commenting on what we were finding.

'What's in this box here?'

'Don't know.'

'Try that one there.'

I picked up a box and opened it carefully. *There'll be food in here for sure.*

'What's in it?'

'Bloody coffee beans.' Neither of us fancied chewing on those, so I threw it back.

When we weren't trying to pick up food, we tried to reassure one another.

'We'll get picked up,' Davey said.

'For sure,' I agreed. '*Laconia*'s crew would have had plenty of time to get a distress signal out before she went down.'

'That's right.'

'There's no harm in this. We'll just sit here and wait.'

'We'll be all right.'

But soon it grew extremely hot because we were near the equator. The morning sun began to sear our faces and arms through the salt and oil that had caked onto our skin. My legs were cool, though. I'd been wearing overalls when I went over the side of *Laconia*, but they weren't on me anymore. I had no idea what happened to them. So my bare legs were dangling in the cool water until I felt the most excruciating pain in my left calf. I drew my legs back onto the raft in a blind panic. At first I thought I'd been bitten by a shark, but the calf had gruesome fang-like puncture marks that made me think it was a barracuda.

Atlantic barracuda can grow up to six feet long. I've never known for sure if that's what bit me, but I certainly know I was in agony. And I've carried the bite marks around with me ever since, as a grim reminder of my time on that raft. The pain was intense and penetrating for a long time before it eased off into a dull, aching numbness.

After that, Davey and I sat back to back on our pathetic little raft with our knees up to our chins, wondering what the hell was going to happen to us. Our sombre thoughts were interrupted by the sudden appearance of an English solider on another raft quite near us. He was in tropical uniform, khaki shirt and shorts, and sitting next to him was a tiny dog. We waved to each other.

'You all right?' we shouted across to him.

'Yes.'

'Seen anybody else?'

'No. There's nobody else around.'

'Thought so.'

'At least I'm sitting on something.'

'Better than swimming,' we agreed.

'Yes. Much better than swimming.' Then he went drifting off and we didn't see him again. We were left with our own thoughts.

'How the hell did he get that dog on board ship?' I asked Davey.

'Buggered if I know. How'd he get it onto the raft?'

'Something to think about, that is.'

'Yeah.'

The day wore on and we didn't see another soul. No one who was alive, anyway. My left leg was badly swollen and aching terribly. We were painfully thirsty and tired, absolutely shattered and drained by what had happened.

Then we heard the same engine-like throbbing we'd heard during the night, but this time it didn't go away and suddenly a sinister shape appeared quite close to us. It was the shape every navy man knew and dreaded. A German U-boat. It was painted a dull green-grey colour and as it got closer we could see the number 156 on its conning tower.

Davey and I didn't say anything. We just sat there on the raft feeling utterly helpless as a group of German sailors emerged from the conning tower and ran along the hull casing toward a large deck gun. Overwhelming terror came over me in a wave of crippling mental agony.

So this is how it's going to end.

We'd been told about atrocities perpetrated by U-boat crews against survivors of the ships they'd torpedoed. Machine-gunning people while they were still in the water was common, we'd been led to believe. As the U-boat crept toward us, diesel engines rumbling, I wanted to curl up into a ball, but I was frozen solid with fear. There was nowhere to hide.

I don't want to die like this.

The U-boat slunk closer and closer, but instead of crashing bullets there came shouts in German. We didn't understand what they were saying but soon realised that the crew hadn't been running to the gun after all. They'd been making for a rope on the bow. They threw it to us and we held on tight while they pulled us alongside their boat.

The relief I felt when I grabbed hold of that rope was

really something special. The terror just slipped away. They pulled us in until our raft was scraping against the curved hull casing, and I saw two or three officers peering down at us from the conning tower. One of them was wearing a white cap with a peak. The others had forage caps.

A couple of sailors reached out to haul us up the sloping side of the submarine, but I couldn't move because of the pain in my leg. So they dragged me carefully over the casing and eased me onto the deck like a limp fish. I could tell by their genuine concern and sympathy as they got us aboard that they were going to treat us well.

The U-boat was quite small, which surprised me. Davey and I were just lying there on its narrow deck, face to face with the German sailors, an enemy we thought we'd never meet, let alone have a group of them help us aboard their U-boat.

I had trouble standing, so several of the sailors half carried me to the base of the conning tower and the narrow steel ladder leading to the top. They motioned that I should climb it.

'You're bloody joking!' I said.

They ignored my protest and gently manhandled me onto the first rung. It was agony, that climb. I don't know how I managed it, but next thing I knew both Davey and I were being bundled over the rim of the conning tower and into its command post. One of the forage-capped officers spoke to us. His English was quite good.

'What are you?' he asked us. 'Italian?'

'No, British.'

'Are you army?'

'No, no,' we said. 'Navy.'

'Your names, please.'

We each gave him our name, rank and serial number. We weren't obliged to tell him more than that and he didn't ask us anything else. He wrote our details down.

Then the officer in the white cap turned to us and, my goodness, he was an impressive looking man. I can see his face quite clearly, even now. It was very lean and tanned, with a deep furrow from an old scar running down one cheek. He had thin lips, a narrow, prominent nose and piercing eyes. They were sharp and very distinctive features. He was the epitome of the German U-boat commander. There was a classic, officer-class look to him. But while he exuded authority and a slight whiff of arrogance, there was a warmth and humanity in his face, which impressed me immensely. His name was Werner Hartenstein, the man who torpedoed *Laconia*. I'll never forget him.

He was wearing an old leather jacket that might have once been brown, but was streaked with green and white from exposure to sea salt. His white officer's cap was battered, and the gold oak leaves around its peak were tarnished green. They were the telltale signs of a man who lived a hard life at sea, exposed to the elements. He spoke to Davey and me in excellent English and with the utmost courtesy.

'So, you are navy?' he asked.

'Yes.'

'Merchant navy or Royal Navy?'

'No, not merchant,' we were quick to tell him. 'Royal Navy.'

'Ah, Royal Navy! Excellent, excellent,' he said, appearing genuinely pleased. 'We'll put you down below. Please don't worry, you will be all right.'

Even though he was the enemy, I instantly liked him and believed what he said.

I stepped through the conning tower hatch with Davey, and climbed down into the bowels of the U-boat. It was dim, cramped and awfully claustrophobic. It reeked of diesel fumes, oil and body odour. The crew directed us to a pokey corner near the boat's two diesel engines. I noticed a metal plate on them that declared they were made in Augsburg. We were in the control room, beneath the conning tower and just to one side. There were a lot of dials and switches and levers. The German sailors controlling the submarine's systems were going about their business efficiently and didn't speak to us at all. From the sound of the engines I got the impression that the boat was slowly under way on the surface.

I sat down beside the vibrating engines and tried to absorb what was going on. It was hard to concentrate. My head felt dull and mushy. The diesel fumes and the way the submarine wallowed in the sea swell was bringing on a dose of seasickness. I'd never felt seasick in my life, so this was something new. Through my dull haze I realised there were other survivors down there with us. They were all filthy, streaked with oil and caked-on salt. I was shocked when it finally sank in that some of them were women. There was a British Fleet Air Arm officer, too. I recognised the wings on his tunic. Those people looked at Davey and me with vacant eyes. They didn't speak to us and we didn't speak to them. We just stared at each other, too exhausted and shocked to do anything.

The crew brought us bread, jam and warm ersatz coffee, but the very sight of food brought me to the verge of vomiting. What an irony. Fifteen minutes earlier I'd been starving and desperate for a drink but, when it came, I felt sick. I had to force myself to eat. I nibbled at the bread and it tasted all right, but the coffee was pretty terrible.

After a while it dawned on me that I was a prisoner-of-war and strangely that didn't upset me at all. I was simply relieved that I was alive and someone would soon look at my leg. I didn't mind the thought of being a prisoner because anything was better than slowly dying on that dreadful raft. My situation became clearer still when the officer who'd taken our names came below and spoke to us again.

'We are going to radio the Vichy French in Dakar,' he told us in his very precise English. 'They will send ships out to this place here. There are other U-boats in the area with us and we are looking for more survivors. We will pick up as many as we can carry. We have found a number of lifeboats. The French will come and they will take you to French North Africa.'

'All right,' we said.

It didn't occur to me that what the Germans were doing was most unusual. U-boats generally didn't bother with picking up survivors. We were the enemy after all. I wasn't in any condition to work it out.

I gradually slid into a semi-comatose state. Physical pain, mental exhaustion, the stench of filthy bodies and the diesel fumes all combined to overwhelm me. I was beyond caring, my mind like mush. We were sunk on the Saturday night, picked up by Hartenstein on Sunday, and it was Wednesday when a German officer came and told us we could go topside for some fresh air. We didn't have to think twice. In a daze I struggled up the conning tower with Davey and, heavens, the air was beautiful up there!

I was astonished to see, astern of U-156, three of *Laconia*'s packed lifeboats, all linked to the submarine by a line. It didn't make sense. Hartenstein was taking a huge risk by remaining on the surface, towing three lifeboats and looking for more survivors, but he didn't seem concerned. The submarine was completely exposed and horribly vulnerable to air attack, yet he was standing there with a pair of binoculars hanging around his neck, eating from a plate heaped with meat and noodles.

'Ah, hello Royal Navy,' he greeted us pleasantly.

'Captain,' we acknowledged.

'You must have this,' he insisted, holding out his plate of food. He urged me to take it. 'Share it with your comrade.'

We were amazed at his generosity in giving up his meal. My appetite had returned, so we gratefully accepted the plate and took it in turns to spoon down the noodles and meat. It was delicious.

'That is better?' Hartenstein asked when we'd finished.

'Yes. Thank you.'

'Good, very good.' He was more than an officer. He was a gentleman. Then, to our surprise, he spoke to us candidly about the sinking while we stood in the confines of his bridge.

'I am very sorry for your situation,' he said, 'but we sighted the gun on your ship's stern and that told us it was an armed merchant ship. We have no alternative but to sink armed merchant ships.'

That bloody gun.

Davey and I exchanged knowing glances, but we weren't about to tell the U-boat commander that we were the crew of the gun he'd seen.

'I was not aware the Italians, our allies, were aboard your ship,' Hartenstein went on. 'I did not know about them or the women and children.'

I felt no resentment toward him as he explained why he had done this to us. I never have. I've always completely understood that it was his duty in a time of war. Then he told us that *Laconia* had broadcast a distress signal and that U-156 had sent out its own messages, in English, asking all ships in the area for help. He confirmed what the other officer had told us, that they had notified the Vichy French and that ships were being sent. So I felt confident we'd be all right.

'With these lifeboats,' Hartenstein said, 'we'll work it in shifts. Some of you people who are on this boat with us will take turns to go back into the lifeboats, and those people will come on board here to have a rest. We will do this until the French come.'

I was enormously impressed by that. He was genuinely concerned for the welfare of the people in the lifeboats, even his enemies. He knew there were women and children in them, exposed to the elements.

After our chat with Hartenstein, he sent us below again, so it was back to the noisy, stinking diesels and the other silent survivors. For a time, Davey and I talked about being prisoners, and then we just watched the crew going about their work. They were fit-looking blokes, those German sailors. They were working hard and continuing to ignore us when a klaxon horn sounded and they started reaching frantically for the levers and switches on their control panels. I just about shot out of my skin. To a sailor, the sound of a klaxon can mean only one thing: something urgent is going on, something big. Orders were being barked out in German. Crewmen were rushing about in the confined space beneath the conning tower. Davey and I stared at each other with widening eyes.

Jesus, what the hell's happening now?

The Fleet Air Arm pilot hurried into the conning tower clutching a hand-held signalling lamp and a white sheet with a red cross on it. The Germans must have given them to him. Then he disappeared and the fear started rising in my throat again. When he came back he spoke to all the survivors.

'There's just been an American aircraft circling overhead,' he explained. He'd flashed a signal to it, saying not to attack because there were survivors from *Laconia* on board. 'It circled and then flew off,' he said. We didn't understand the significance of that and he didn't elaborate.

We soon saw him make a dash for the conning tower again, and he had just disappeared from view when there was an ear-splitting explosion. The U-boat seemed to lift straight up and then fall down again. It was an incredibly violent movement. Then the entire boat started shaking. Brisk, sharp commands were being exchanged among the crew.

Oh, please, no. Dear God, not again!

I couldn't believe what was happening. Then there was another explosion and the U-boat leapt and shook again. My ears were ringing and I was close to choking on my own fear. Through it all I connected the circling American aircraft with the explosions. We were being bombed.

'Raus! Raus!' The Germans began yelling at us. 'Raus!' They were pointing to the conning tower. I knew we had to get out but I didn't want to go. I was safe. I had food. I wanted to stay right where I was, thank you very much.

Davey and I got to our feet and the crew started pushing us up the ladder inside the conning tower. I couldn't move quickly because of the pain in my leg, but I got to the top somehow and Hartenstein was there.

'I cannot jeopardise the boat,' he said urgently. 'You must go. We are damaged and we are going to dive. Go, go!'

From the conning tower I thought the U-boat was a little down at the bow. The deck was awash. There was a large group of other survivors splashing along the deck and diving overboard. There was no sign of the American aircraft.

I looked astern for the three lifeboats, but I could only see two of them. I didn't know it then, but the third lifeboat, the middle one, had taken a direct hit from a bomb. It had been full of people. I would have to swim to the remaining lifeboats and they had already drifted hundreds of yards away from the stern.

Davey disappeared over the edge of the conning tower. I never saw him again. I half climbed, half fell down the ladder on the outside of the tower until I reached the deck.

I stumbled to the edge, dived overboard and started swimming for my life again.

That was a dreadful swim. It was the hardest physical thing I've ever had to do in my life. I set my sights on one of the lifeboats in the distance and swam for it with a frantic energy I didn't know I possessed. I was totally exhausted before I started out, and I didn't think I could do it, but a desperate kind of strength emerged from somewhere. The swell was quite big and it was punishing me, thrusting me up and backwards the moment I felt I'd made a bit of progress. It was hard to keep a rhythm going, but I kept focusing on the lifeboat in the distance and thrashed away at the water with my arms and legs. *This isn't happening.* I simply couldn't grasp that I was in the water again, struggling to survive for the second time. It just didn't seem real. My entire body was shrieking with pain and my left leg felt as if it belonged to someone else. I went on like that for more than half an hour.

When I finally reached the boat I'd been aiming for, I found a desperate crowd of other swimmers already there. They were clinging to the ropes that were looped along the gunwale. The boat was already hopelessly overcrowded. People were standing up, shoulder to shoulder. I couldn't see how they would fit me in, but I couldn't go anywhere else. I couldn't swim another stroke.

But those already in the boat had different ideas. 'Can't get any more in here,' they were yelling. 'Too full.'

'Pull me in!' I begged.

Some of them were roughly pushing the people in the water away from the boat. A sailor who'd been part of our navy contingent on *Laconia* was peering over the edge, carefully surveying all the soggy bundles of humanity clinging to the side. His name was Gibson.

'One of ours here!' he suddenly called out. 'One of ours here, I'm taking him in.'

Through a blur of exhaustion I realised he was looking at me when he said that, and then strong hands pulled me into the bow of the lifeboat. I was a dead weight after that swim, so utterly exhausted I couldn't move a muscle. I just wanted to lie down and go to sleep, but I couldn't because there was no room. So I stood. That boat was absolutely packed with what I can only describe as human wreckage. We were all filthy, covered in oil, soaking wet and shaking with fear.

We began to drift away from the poor souls still struggling in the water, leaving them to face certain death. As we huddled together in the lifeboat with no room to move, everything fell silent. There was an overpowering sense of disbelief and shock. Our situation seemed utterly hopeless.

Within minutes of me being pulled into the lifeboat, U-156 rumbled alongside. I was surprised that she was still on the surface, given the bombing attack by the Americans. Hartenstein was leaning over the rim of the conning tower.

'Take up a course north-north-east. That is the direction of the coast of Africa. It is seven hundred miles away,' he said. 'I'm sorry but I cannot give you any food.'

No one said anything back to him. We were too shocked, too stunned. Seven hundred miles to the nearest land! It was just too much to absorb, totally crushing.

Then Hartenstein brought himself to attention and

saluted us, a solitary figure in his conning tower, showing us the greatest possible respect.

'I do not think you will make it,' he called out. 'But good luck to all of you.'

And that was my last glimpse of Commander Werner Hartenstein. U-156 pulled away and I didn't see it dive. At that moment, Hartenstein's U-boat seemed like an apparition to me, a dream. It just faded away.

Then there was just the lifeboat and our one common enemy, the sea. The sea, by its very nature, does not distinguish between friend and foe. It is forever the irreconcilable enemy of ships and men. I was about to discover what a cruel enemy it could be.

I was 12 when this photo
was taken

My class at HMS *Drake*, 1939.
Back row, from left: Johnny Hennessey, self, Charlie Hughes.
Middle row, extreme left: Peter Rimmer. Third from right: Freddie Powell.
Front centre: Hicks

HMS *Valiant*, as she appeared when I joined her in 1939
(Photograph: US Naval Historical Center)

On board HMS *Valiant*, next to a 15-inch gun turret.
I am standing on the right

RMS *Laconia*

Werner Hartenstein, commander of U-156
(Photograph: Horst Bredow, U-boot Archiv)

Lifeboat overflowing with *Laconia* survivors
(Photograph: Horst Bredow, U-boot Archiv)

U-506 with lifeboat full of survivors
(Photograph: Horst Bredow, U-boot Archiv)

Laconia survivors on the deck of U-156
(Photograph: Horst Bredow, U-boot Archiv)

Able Seaman Jim McLoughlin, RN

Moorsburne,
Pembroke Road,
Woking,
Surrey
4.2.44

Dear Mr. McLoughlan,

Thank you very much indeed for your charming letter which I was so glad to receive. I was glad too, to hear news of your son, with whom I shared so much. He was always wonderfully patient, cheerful & helpful. & so kind & considerate of me all the time. I was truly glad that he was able to stand the strain physically & mentally so that he at last reached you safely. I wasn't able to do very much for them all but in times like that perhaps mer

Letter from Doris Hawkins to my father, 4 February, 1944
(part 1)

rely on women's faith & encouragement
more than one can ever realise.

I should very much like to
meet your son again some day &
when I visit Liverpool I should certainly
like to call & see you too, if I may.

I am sending you two copies
of *Atlantic Torpedo*, with my very best
wishes. Will you be so kind as to
send one on to James, please? I should
so much like to know what he thinks
of it. I never intended to write a book,
but so very many people asked me
to do so & finally I did, and it has
been very kindly received.

I am now back at my
profession, doing full time nursing as
Sister in the Maternity Department of my
own hospital – St. Thomas's, which is
evacuated from London to Woking for the
duration.

(part 2)

Thank you again for writing.

Yours very sincerely,
Doris M. Hawkins

Morrisburne,
Pembroke Road,
Woking,
Surrey
5. 2. 44.

Dear "McLoughlin",

I automatically write the familiar name by which I knew you in those days & nights during which we tossed on the Atlantic, but somehow I feel that back in civilisation "James" would be more suitable.

It was so kind of your father to write, & I was very, very glad to hear of you again. I am sending you a copy of the booklet which I was persuaded to write. I think that I am glad now that I have done it as it seems to have helped many people. Do let me know what you think of it, & whether it

Letter from Doris Hawkins to me, 5 February, 1944
(part 1)

gives a true picture of our experiences for you too.

If you have the addresses of any of the other survivors do please let me know & I will send each a copy.

I am glad to hear that you are well & working again — So am I, but I never forget, & I am sure you cannot either.

I hope that one day we shall meet again — you were always so kind & helpful to me & always looked after me whenever possible, & I am so grateful for those memories in the midst of many that I would rather not have.

With the very best of good wishes

Yours very sincerely,

Doris M. Hawkins

"Freckles"

(part 2)

ATLANTIC TORPEDO

The record of 27 days
in an open boat
following   U-boat sinking

By the only woman survivor

DORIS M. HAWKINS

S.R.N., S.C.M.

1/-

Original copy of Doris Hawkins' book, *Atlantic Torpedo*

Dorothy Field, WRNS, 1944

At HMS *Golden Hind*,
Sydney, 1945

Graduation photo, Police Training Course, Falfield, 1948.
I am in the front row, far left

In front of the Police House,
Harbertonford Village, Devon, 1954

Doris M Hawkins OBE (1911–1991)
(Photograph: courtesy Mrs Norah King, via
Shaun Tyas/Paul Watkins Publishing)

6

Our grim struggle begins

At first, nothing happened. A terrible silence overcame us with only the sound of the Atlantic swell as a desolate background to our misery.

I was appalled at how crowded the lifeboat was. Many of us were standing shoulder to shoulder, so jam-packed that even with the sea swell rolling beneath us, there was no chance of falling over. Others were sitting crammed together on the thwarts, the bench-like seats that ran across the boat, while even more were lying down in the water that was slopping around the bilges. They didn't seem to notice.

At first I didn't give their welfare the slightest thought. I was too exhausted and frightened. Before night threw its black Atlantic blanket over us, my only concern was for me, and my feelings of loneliness and despair. Nothing else. The powerful force of self-preservation that had surged through me during the desperate leap from the U-boat and propelled me during the painful swim to the lifeboat was still very much with me.

At least I'm still alive, and I've got a boat under me again.

The rest of that dreadful afternoon and the first night in the lifeboat passed in a blur of shock and deeply draining fatigue. The sun went down and we were quickly chilled to the bone. The sea made an endless, depressing slap, slap, slap against the wooden hull. I slipped into a dream-like world of distorted human shapes, muffled groans and half-heard snippets of conversation. If I slept at all it must have been on my feet because in the morning I was still standing.

With the first rays of morning sun a small, tentative buzz of life ran through the boat and people started to organise themselves. A handful set about organising others. In the meantime, everyone was squirming and elbowing a little more private space for themselves. For some reason we weren't jammed so tightly together, so we could move about a little easier. I was still too shocked to consider why some empty spaces were suddenly there.

I wasn't too pleased by the other survivors around me. They were mostly old people. That, at least, was how they appeared to me. A few were sailors around my age, but the majority were in their 40s. Some were a great deal older. I was just a kid compared to them, someone of little consequence. I felt even more lonely than I had before. I started to miss Davey and wondered what had become of him.

'How many of us are here, do you think?' someone asked.

'Don't know. Could be fifty or so.'

'We should do a head count.'

There were 64 British men, two British women and two Polish officer cadets. Sixty-eight people crammed into one 30-foot boat. One of the women, a Scot whose name was Mary, was in a bad way, with skin peeling away from her face in long strips. The other was Doris Hawkins, a stout, robust nurse with a friendly, round face. It was an extraordinary collection of people, which included a number of civilians and various ranks of the three services. There was a lieutenant colonel of the British Army, a squadron leader, a pilot officer and a number of sergeants from the RAF, the Fleet Air Arm officer who had been on the submarine, and several of *Laconia*'s crew, including her bosun, chief petty officer, assistant purser, assistant engineer and electrician. *Laconia*'s surgeon, Doctor Geoffrey Purslow, was there too.

A mere handful of these people have stayed alive in my memory for more than 60 years. I can still see some of their faces and sometimes, in the dead of night, I hear their voices. But the majority have never been anything more than a blur to me, especially the older, more senior officers who kept together and had no reason to speak to an able seaman like me. And many others who perished so quickly, which has deeply troubled and haunted me ever since.

The sun hadn't been up long when we heard an aircraft approaching. My stomach lurched. We waited with a mix of mounting fear and hope while a black speck emerged from the pink morning sky and grew into a large four-engine aircraft. It was flying very low. When it banked steeply over us, we could see the American insignia on the fuselage and wings, and a relieved murmur ran through the lifeboat. A signal lamp winked at us from the aircraft but no one, not even the Fleet Air Arm Officer, could read it. We stirred into a bout of yelling, frantically waving our arms and odd bits of clothing above our heads. I privately allowed myself a small measure of hope and confidence. At that point I didn't think about dying.

This is a good thing, Jim. They know where we are and they'll send help. It shouldn't be very long, maybe just a day or two for a ship to reach us.

After it had flown several low circles around us, the aircraft flew off, leaving us alone in the Atlantic swell. After it had gone, the officers took stock of our situation with a sense of urgency, and soon discovered that we had precious little at our disposal. There were a number of oars, a knife and a few other odd tools, a tin of putty-like white lead, a few bailing tins, a bucket, some odd bits of rope, a paltry number of life jackets and a compass. The compass was fixed in the stern near the tiller. There were no sails, but there were two blankets and a filthy little triangle of yellow canvas. There were no medical supplies.

The rations were pathetically meagre for 68 people: some Horlicks tablets, a small supply of chocolate, a few tins of Pemmican, which was a food spread that looked a bit like Vegemite, and several tins of biscuits that were as hard as a dog's head. Most significantly, though, there were just 15 gallons of water in the boat's water tank, not anywhere near enough for us all on a voyage of 700 miles in the heat of the tropics.

I was shocked and angry about this cruel shortage of life-sustaining food and water. The rations stowed aboard all ships' lifeboats were always substantial, so I knew that our boat had been raided by pilferers, either people aboard *Laconia* or dock workers in Britain or some foreign port she had visited. Such behaviour was rife because wartime restrictions meant that food was often in short supply. Emergency provisions in lifeboats, it seemed, were fair game and we were faced with the deadly proof. We could live for a great many days without food, but there would be no hope whatsoever once the water was gone.

We were quickly galvanised into action by the officers, who had gathered in the stern.

'We must set a course and get moving,' they said. 'It's pointless hanging around hoping for rescue or a miracle. The German captain said north-north-east and seven hundred miles, so we'd better start rowing. Those who are physically able will have to take their turn at the oars.'

The responsibility for rowing fell mainly to the sailors, which was only natural, so we quickly got ourselves organised into shifts. I welcomed the chance to row because it would not only help take my mind off things, but also give me the chance to sit down at last. Someone made room for me on one of the thwarts, I gripped an oar and began to heave away.

I felt a bit better once I started rowing on that first day. It gave me a sense of purpose, because we couldn't afford to drift aimlessly about. We had to get a move on. It was hard, muscle-wrenching work and although we were making slow progress, I didn't say anything. I just kept rowing. In the stern, the chief petty officer sat at the tiller, eyes fixed on the compass, pointing us in the general direction of Africa.

There wasn't much to say when the rowing started. Those of us at the oars were too busy concentrating on keeping our rhythm. We moved along smoothly while the sailors were all rowing on the same shift, but when a few army types and civilians took up the oars, it got a bit erratic. I tried to show them how to do it, coaching them in the same way our instructors had done at HMS *Drake*.

'Grip the oars like this, no further apart than the width of your shoulders. Then it's a smooth semi-circular motion. Dip the oar into the water, pull back strongly, lift it out, feather the blade, then dip it back in again. In, pull, out, feather, in, pull, out, feather, in ...' A few of them got the hang of it, but others were just plain hopeless.

During one of my stints at the oars a civilian chap sat facing me. He had black hair and was wearing a shirt and sports jacket, as if he'd just got dressed for a leisurely game of deck tennis on a cruise ship. There was something odd about the way he was sitting. The boat was pitching and rolling in the swell, yet he wasn't hanging on to anything. He just sat there, lolling listlessly with his hands hanging between his knees.

'I can't row,' he said to me.

It wasn't an excuse or an apology, more a dull statement of fact. I couldn't think of anything to say to him. I just kept the rhythm on my oar. *In, pull, out, feather, in ...* But after a little while he spoke to me again.

'It's my hands,' he said, and showed me his palms. He didn't appear to have any. Instead he had two bloody, pulpy masses of raw meat attached to each wrist, with stringy lifeless fingers jutting out from them. I stared and felt my stomach turn over. *In, pull, out, feather, in ...*

'What happened?' I asked.

'I went over the side of the ship on a rope. Slid all the way down to the water.'

At HMS *Drake* they had taught us how to put a rope between our legs and ease our way down, hand over hand. We got good at it with a bit of practice, but it was drummed into us that we should never, ever let the rope slide through our hands. Rope burn is cruel.

'I can't row,' he said again.

The poor man had spent many hours in salt water mixed with oil. I couldn't even imagine the agony he must have been in. With no medical supplies, Doctor Purslow wasn't able to do anything for him. There was certainly nothing I could do, except pity him and silently admire the fact that he didn't complain, not once. He wasn't the only one suffering, though. Others in the boat were nursing all kinds of injuries, deep gashes on arms and legs, angry bruises, scraped and cruelly torn skin.

But the day wore on regardless. The rowers kept rowing. There was a bad leak somewhere, so those who couldn't take a turn at the oars were kept busy bailing water out of the bilges. *Laconia*'s engineer and the bosun eventually found the leak when they removed two of the boat's buoyancy tanks. Those two chaps were real old salts, veterans of improvisation after decades spent at sea in the merchant navy. They pulled fibres from one of the pieces of rope we had on board and mixed them with some white lead to create a glue-like mixture, which they then worked in between the troublesome timbers. From then on we didn't have to bail nearly as often.

To get at the buoyancy tanks they had to remove the wooden doors that covered them. After they fixed the leak, the two old salts placed the doors across the bottom of the boat amidships, to form makeshift floorboards, which gave the nurse Doris Hawkins and Mary their own dry space in which to lie down. Then the engineer turned one of the remaining doors into a sign by fashioning the letters *SOS Water* onto it with white lead.

'We'll be needing that signal,' he said optimistically. 'They'll be sending ships and aeroplanes out to us.'

By the middle of the first day I knew that we wouldn't be able to keep rowing long enough to reach land. It was a forlorn hope. The heat was unbelievable. Without any shade, the sun had a searing double edge to it, burning us from above and then reflecting wildly off the waves to fry us from below. Our throats were parched, but the officers had decided we would have to wait until six o'clock before we could have our first ration of water.

We only stopped rowing and rested as the sun went down. Then the officers distributed our rations and they had no option but to be miserly in the extreme. We each received what amounted to about one tablespoon of water. It got passed along to us, hand-to-hand, in an oblong ration tin. After taking my shifts at the oars I was so thirsty that my tongue was sticking to the roof of my mouth. Our tongues had already begun to swell. When it came my turn to drink, I tilted the tin so that the precious water collected in the corner. I brought the tin to my parted lips but there was no relief. It felt as though the water soaked straight into the inside of my mouth, and was gone before I even had a chance to swallow it. Then a few of the hard biscuits were broken up into tiny pieces and passed around. I held my little piece in my mouth until it became soft enough to chew. I had great difficulty swallowing it, though. It got stuck at regular intervals on the way down. Others leant over the side and dipped their fragment of biscuit into the sea in an attempt to soften it. After that some chocolate and Horlicks tablets were distributed. I couldn't eat the Horlicks. It was sticky from the heat and quite revolting.

By the time we'd finished our rations it was dark and the temperature plummeted. The sudden cold brought on a deep, pulsing pain in my leg where I'd been bitten. A few of us picked up the oars again to keep warm, and the night passed in a blur of aching muscles and horrible moans coming from various parts of the boat. My chin kept dropping to my chest as I rowed, but I still maintained the steady, hypnotic rower's rhythm. *In, pull, out, feather, in . . .* I thought at one stage I heard a disturbance followed by a splash, then convinced myself I must have drifted off to sleep at the oars and dreamt it.

The next day was pretty much the same. And the day after that. The only difference was that the pain in our arms got worse, our tongues got larger and the sun grew hotter. I kept hearing strange scuffles and splashes during the night and each morning the boat was roomier.

On the third night, a few of us kept rowing again. Everyone else slumped into uneasy sleep. We heard the throb of diesel engines approaching and the familiar shape of a submarine loomed out of the darkness. It drew up right alongside and a group of officers shouted from the conning tower:

'Italiano? Italiano?'

The noise of the submarine and the shouting stirred the people who had been asleep.

'What the bloody hell's going on?'

'It's another German U-boat.'

'No, no, I think they're saying they're Italians.'

'Germans, Italians, what's the bleedin' difference? Unless they've got some rum, tell the buggers to piss off,' an irritated, half-asleep sailor said from the stern of the lifeboat.

'Italiano? Italiano?'

'I reckon they're asking about Italian survivors.'

'No, no Italians here,' we yelled back at them.

That reply seemed to satisfy them and the officers disappeared into the conning tower. The submarine rumbled off and vanished into the night.

7
Drifting into madness

I don't know how long that little incident took to play itself out, but it seemed one minute we were alone, the next there was an Italian submarine beside us, and then it was gone. It was so utterly surreal and incomprehensible that no one in our boat said anything after the Italians had gone. The rowers started rowing again, while the others retreated into their drowsiness. We had been through so much that the Italians' blatant disregard didn't sink into our numb minds. There was just a silent acceptance that they were looking for their fellow countrymen, not us. After that, Hartenstein's courage and compassion was all the more impressive in my mind.

The next day we rowed some more, but it became utterly exhausting. Every part of my body was jumping and twitching with pain. I had huge, red raw circular sores on my buttocks from chaffing on the wet timber thwart as I rowed. My hands were blistered and had started oozing a pappy, fleshy muck. Salt-water boils were breaking out all over me, and my tongue was lodged in my throat like a dead lizard. My lips were split and bleeding and I was so sunburnt that every bit of exposed flesh was drawn as tight as a drum. The pores of my skin were covered in a thin veil of salt. I had no urge to urinate and, although it was terribly hot, I wasn't sweating. Everyone else was suffering in similar ways. Only a few days had passed and we were already rapidly deteriorating. The moaning in the boat increased and the dreadful sound of people suffering began eating away at my resolve. It was agonising to hear people dying slowly of thirst, exhaustion and despair.

One by one our small group of rowers grew weaker, with each of us spending shorter and shorter spells at the oars. The heat and lack of water was sapping our strength and, seeing this, the bosun worked out a way to make us a small sail. I'm filled with admiration for the way he did it, like a magician creating something out of nothing. He took one of the oars and, using the oddments of rope we had, secured it in an upright position even though there wasn't a fitting for it in the bottom of the boat. Then he rigged the yellow triangle of canvas to it. We watched anxiously and were delighted to see this pitifully small makeshift sail catch the slight breeze and begin to swell. A moment or two later we felt the boat moving of its own accord.

'Thank Christ for that,' croaked one of the rowers.

'Hear, hear,' another agreed.

In the stern, the chief petty officer worked away at the tiller to keep the sail at its best angle to the breeze as he held his course. It was wonderful to hear the bow moving through the water without rowing. For a few more days we occasionally took to the oars if there wasn't enough wind to keep us moving, but soon we were too weak to do even that. We gave up rowing completely and no one seemed to care that we'd stopped.

Instead, we directed our scant remaining energy to

creating some desperately needed pockets of shade. We secured the oars across the boat, from gunwale to gunwale, and spread the two blankets and odd bits of spare clothing over them. We'd take turns to crawl beneath this ramshackle shelter to find some small measure of relief from the worst of the tropical sun. Then, when night came, we'd have to reclaim our ragged clothing and wrap it around us to ward off the cold. We were never completely dry, even in the blast-furnace heat of the day. There was always water splashing about in the bottom of the boat, so when night fell, the chill invaded us quickly. On other occasions, two or three men held the blankets in a circle around Doris and Mary, so those two gentle, modest women could relieve themselves in private using the bucket. For the men who could still urinate, it was so much easier. They just did it over the side. As the days drifted by, no one took any notice or cared.

I looked forward to the mornings. When the sun first came up and before the heat began in earnest, a fine rain would occasionally engulf the boat. It was what sailors call a sea fret. It would usually only last a few minutes, but what bliss it was. We would lie back with our mouths open as wide as our painfully cracked lips would allow, just to catch a few precious drops of water. The sea fret had a slightly salty taste, but it was nectar to us. Anything that supplemented our scant store of water gave us hope that we might just make it all the way to Africa.

But while some mornings brought this precious gift of water, the dawn light also revealed people lying dead in the bottom of our boat. Doctor Purslow, himself growing visibly weaker, would struggle over to them and, with sorrow and great compassion, hold their hands and feel their wrists in search of a pulse, then sadly shake his head.

'Looks like he's gone,' he'd say, his voice breaking with emotion. The poor man was in torment because he was a doctor and there was nothing at all he could do.

At other times Doris would check on the motionless bundles. If she wasn't sure they were dead, she would rub their faces and hands in the hope that she could stimulate their blood flow. Occasionally one of the lifeless forms would stir at her touch and slowly rally to endure another day. But if she declared it pointless, the poor wretches were lifted over the side and lowered reverently into the water. At first someone would recall a few meaningful words from the Bible, or something else that seemed appropriate. Eventually, though, we ran out of things to say and just watched them float away or sink as we retreated into our own misery. Their legacy was more room to stretch out or lie down, more clothes to stretch over the oars to create more shade, and more water for those of us remaining.

Water became an obsession. When our rations were passed around each night, as the sun was setting, we found ways of making our precious tablespoon of water last as long as possible. But all too soon it was swallowed and the thirst seemed worse than before. When we managed to talk, we fantasised about sipping glasses of ice-cold water and spoke with deep regret about all the water we'd taken for granted and wasted over the years.

'I'll never waste another drop,' someone would vow. 'Never, ever.'

'How could I have left the tap running every time I brushed my teeth? Oh for just one handful of that water now.'

'Just think,' Doris said. 'People in England are mopping floors with buckets of water while we're bobbing about out here.'

One day we noticed the two Polish officer cadets leaning over the side. They each scooped up a handful of sea water and drank it.

'You're stark raving bloody mad. Don't drink the sea water, it'll kill you!' we challenged them.

'Is all right,' one of the brothers said. 'For us is all right. We can do this.'

'Bollocks! Everyone knows you can't drink sea water.'

'Is all right for us,' the Poles insisted. 'But not you, no. Will kill you, not us.'

This set off a heated discussion about the pros and cons of drinking sea water. It was very, very tempting, because in the daytime the sea looked so clear, cool and refreshing. Then the Poles managed in their halting English to explain what they meant.

'Once, we work in Russia. In salt mine. All the drinking water very salty. We get used to it. Little by little, used to it. Is okay if we drink a little sea water, but not you. It kills you.'

As extraordinary as this explanation seemed, we took them at their word and waited in mounting desperation for our nightly water ration. At first the rations were scrupulously issued by the senior officers, but these older men were among the first to grow weak and soon there were none left. Authority died with them, and another small group got together in the stern, taking control of what little we had. I won't say what service those men were from, but from that time our numbers fell quite quickly. We were going through a sort of natural culling. It's a dreadful way of putting it, I know, but that's just how it was. The weak were dying, the strong were hanging on. But, if I was any indication, only just.

However, a secretive corner of my brain whispered that things weren't right and that, even though we were in dire straits, people were dying far too quickly. I was still hearing what I believed to be muted struggles and muffled cries in the aching chill of night. A deep and dark sense of foreboding invaded me. It mingled incessantly with my thirst, hunger and exhaustion, and I looked furtively at my fellow survivors. Many were fraying at the edges. Then I became preoccupied with how I was looking. I felt like death and wondered if I looked like it. I didn't want to look like death. I wanted to look strong and worthy of the water that the group in the stern was dishing out. Hope was dwindling in proportion to the amount of water left.

One night, the makeshift sail was flapping pathetically in the slightest of breezes and the Atlantic was making its ceaseless slap, slap, slap against the hull. The boat was its usual nightmare of vague shapes, moans and half-mad mutterings. Everyone looked like a ghost. I was in the bow as usual. It was my spot and I rarely moved from it. The chief petty officer was resting. The Fleet Air Arm chap had taken his place at the tiller and was keeping us on course until, for no apparent reason, he stood bolt upright and began singing.

'Show me the way to go home!' he bellowed.

'Shut up!'

'Show me the way to go home, I'm tired and I want to go to bed,' the officer sang on. 'I had a little drink about an hour ago, and it's gone right to my head.'

Mad bastard.

Of course, that's exactly what he was, mad. This poor young officer's mind had completely broken and he just kept singing in a rowdy, demented fashion. Then, without any warning whatsoever, he jumped overboard and drifted into the night, still singing loudly.

'Show me the way to go home, show me the way to go home.'

There was a mad scramble at the stern.

'Quick, get hold of the tiller,' a shaken voice yelled.

'I've got it!' the chief cried out, then added almost as an afterthought: 'Well, that's another one gone.'

It didn't really make a lot of difference, hurrying to get hold of the tiller. It wasn't as if we were in a speeding motor launch.

Knowing that one of us had actually gone mad scared the hell out of me. It really shook me. My mind began racing.

How long before we're all driven crazy? Will the end be quiet and peaceful, or will it come in a ranting torrent of madness?

The chief quickly realised that the compass wasn't working. The Fleet Air Arm officer had broken it to get at the vital alcohol it contained. He had, indeed, had a little drink about an hour ago. From then on we had to navigate by the sun during the day and the stars at night. This was a shocking blow that spread a further pall of fear and uncertainty through the boat. I could hear people sobbing.

After that terrifying episode I loathed the darkness. I associated it with going mad. It was never totally dark, though. I don't recall there being any moonlight, but the eerie phosphorescence of the sea gave the boat and its occupants an unreal, spirit-like appearance that I found terribly disturbing. Everything took on a nightmarish quality, my imagination started running wild and I became filled with dread. In some ways total blackness would have been preferable.

The breeze would sometimes get up a bit at night, triggering unidentifiable scrapes, sudden thuds and relentless tapping noises that drove me to the point of screaming. I sat there in the bow, lonely and alert as restless shapes stirred and moaned, wondering who would go mad next, who would be dead in the morning.

Over the next few nights, several people stood up quietly, climbed over the side without a fuss, let go of the gunwale and disappeared. No one tried to stop them. We just watched them without a word. We certainly didn't blame them because each of us, in our own way, understood that we couldn't withstand much more of this.

The nights also brought a new and alarming worry crowding in on me. I had visions of my family receiving the worst possible news from the Admiralty, that my ship had been sunk, and I was feared lost at sea. I could see the anguish on their faces, the tears in their eyes. This tormented me, knowing that I was the cause of such a terrible shock to them. *Maybe they don't know anything about* Laconia *yet, and are going about their lives thinking*

I'm all right when in fact I'm stuck in this damn boat. Maybe they don't know anything. They might not know for years. I wanted to apologise to them. Then the daylight would come, perhaps with another sea fret depositing moisture on our faces, and our situation seemed a little less desperate.

I was having trouble distinguishing one day from another. I had counted the first three days, but after that everything became wildly scattered in my mind. *How long has it been now? Let me think ... a week already? No, no, it must be at least two weeks, surely.* The comfort of time had vanished.

With each day, and each death, the boat grew quieter. There was very little conversation as we all retreated into our own private, tormented worlds. I spent a great deal of time leaning on the gunwales just watching the empty sea. One day I saw an albatross soaring effortlessly from wave to wave on its magnificent wings and it made me understand the anguish in those words Coleridge wrote in *The Rhyme of the Ancient Mariner*:

'Water, water everywhere and not a drop to drink.'

The sea was a beautiful, greenish-blue colour, so fresh and cool-looking that it was tempting to jump in. In the beginning, some people had actually cooled off in that way from time to time. Doris believed that by keeping wet, our bodies might absorb desperately needed moisture, but there was no way I was going in there. I'd already been bitten once, so I was well-satisfied with simply staring into the water, daydreaming about fish and chips and cups of tea.

There were always plenty of pilot fish darting about, feeding off the weed and slime that invariably grows on the bottom of boats. There'd been a number of farcical attempts at catching them. One of the sailors, a bloke from Birmingham called Brom, saw himself as a bit of a fisherman. He was absolutely determined to catch a pilot fish. He pulled away a length of the wire that ran around the boat underneath the gunwhale and, using his knife, fashioned a hook from a piece of one of our flimsy biscuit tins. He lashed the hook to the end of the wire and stood up to lower his makeshift fishing line over the side with great ceremony.

'I'll catch us all something tasty,' he declared solemnly.

'Of course you will, Brom.' We didn't believe him for a minute.

'I will, you see if I don't.'

The next moment there was a tremendous upheaval of water beside the boat and a bloody great whale surfaced right next to us! It was the most magnificent creature, a blue whale, and it was absolutely massive. And there was Brom, standing with his fishing line poised and his eyes popping out of his head as he tried to keep his balance in the wildly rocking boat.

'What did I tell you!' he yelled. 'I caught us the biggest bloody fish you ever saw.' We all laughed.

The whale just lay there on the surface for a bit, eyeing us off. Maybe it thought our boat was another whale because it really did give us the once over.

'How you going to get it on board, eh Brom?'

'And when you get it on board, how are you going to carve it up evenly?'

The magnificent creature lay beside us in the water a

little longer, calmly watching us. And then it dived. Goodness, that was something I'll never forget, seeing it go under. As it headed for the deep, its tail flukes arched out of the water in the most majestic way and came down again with an almighty wack on the surface. The sea erupted, the boat rocked alarmingly and then the huge creature was gone. And there stood Brom with his makeshift fishing line still poised in the air.

'Ah, you let it get away Brom!' someone complained. 'Call yourself a fisherman, do you?'

It soon dawned on us that we'd actually had a lucky escape. If the whale's tail had come down on top of us, it would have smashed the boat to pieces. Or if it had gone underneath the boat it would have capsized us in an instant and we would have been done for, right there and then.

We never did catch any fish. We saw flying fish on most days, though, beautiful creatures that leapt out of the water for short, sparkling flights on elegant gossamer wings. When two of them surprised us by flying straight into the boat, they were immediately set upon, killed, and pulled apart by eager hands. A few people ate little pieces of them, but I was beyond being hungry and couldn't face it. Someone managed to manhandle a squid into the bottom of the boat, but it was revoltingly jelly-like and oozed a disgusting black substance. No one wanted to touch it, let alone eat it. Even our pathetic rations were more inviting than this, so we threw it back over the side.

A day or two after our rendezvous with the blue whale, one of the sailors near me stirred.

'I think I see a ship,' he said.

I heard those words vaguely through a wall of heat and lethargy. I peered out from beneath the shelter of ragged clothing.

'Are you sure?'

'Over there, look.'

'Jesus, it's a ship all right,' another sailor said, and I looked at where he was pointing.

'Three funnels,' I said.

'Which way is it going?'

'Can't tell.'

Suspense rose in the boat as everyone stirred and focussed on this marvellous shape that was shimmering on the horizon like a mirage. We watched and waited in silence and the shape kept getting bigger until it was clear that she would cut across us at a bit of an angle.

'They'll see us.'

'Bound to.'

'That's the *Britannic*,' I said.

'Do you think?'

'Pretty sure. She was in Cape Town when *Laconia* called in there. I remember her shape.'

'What is she?'

'A liner. A Cunard White Star ship.'

When the ship got to within three or four miles of our boat, we started waving our hands and bits of clothing, anything to attract attention. We stuffed a lifejacket into the ladies' toilet bucket and set fire to it using a petrol cigarette lighter that, by some miracle, still worked. Thick black smoke billowed into the air, but it was useless. The liner didn't alter course or slow and soon we were looking at her stern in despair. Eventually she vanished over the horizon. It was heart wrenching.

'She didn't bloody well stop.'

'She didn't see us,' I remarked flatly. 'We're a tiny boat, low down in the water. It would've been a miracle if she'd seen us.'

8

Ruthless measures

Deep inside I was raging as *Britannic* disappeared. The Germans had a strategy of keeping U-boats near where they'd sunk a ship, hoping to torpedo any rescue vessels. If by some slim chance *Britannic* had seen us and stopped, she would have been a sitting duck. It was dreadful seeing possible rescue slip away from us like that. An overwhelming sense of desolation engulfed us and I think this had a profound effect on some of those who were barely hanging on. No one spoke for the rest of the day.

Perhaps a day or two after we saw that ship, Mary the Scotswoman faded away from us. She was such a lovely person, a kind and very gracious lady of about 40. She lay slumped across the lap of Doris, who cradled her head like a child's, gently stroking her hair. My God, that was sad. She'd been an uncomplaining stalwart, sitting amidships quietly day after day with Doris. They never left each other's side, drawing strength from one another in their terribly difficult situation as the only women on board. Mary always spoke with the utmost courtesy to everyone around her. But she had clearly given up and was wordlessly slipping away. Then, the next morning, Doris couldn't wake her and announced that she was dead. Doctor Purslow conducted a little service for her.

He led us in prayer and we tried to sing a hymn, but our voices just petered out with sadness and exhaustion. After that, she was lowered into the Atlantic.

Dreadfully alone without Mary, Doris moved to the bow of the boat where I was ensconced with a couple of other navy blokes and a young chap from the RAF. She became a mother figure to us in the bow, watching over us, I suppose because she was a nurse and had a natural instinct for caring for others. I started to call her Freckles because the relentless sun had brought her round face out in a wild rash of browny-red freckles. I guess I was a bit impertinent to do that, but she didn't seem to mind in the slightest. She always called me McLoughlin, never James or Jim or Mac.

Doris confided in me that she was terribly worried about Geoffrey Purslow. He was an extraordinary man. I can only guess how old he was, but I'd say about 30. Older than me, of course, but quite a bit younger than many of the others. A slight man with very pale skin, he had the quiet, confident air of the medical professional about him. As *Laconia*'s surgeon he would have had a big responsibility for such a relatively young man. That pressure must have been greater in the lifeboat, because he had nothing with which to help us, except his own humanity and compassion. He was the only one who constantly moved about the boat, going from person to person, encouraging us. He used his tiny pen knife to burst blisters, lance ulcers and release the painful pressure in septic toes and fingers. Some of those sores were quite disgusting, oozing vile puss and infected blood.

In the days following the death of Mary, Purslow slipped into rapid decline. Like all of us, he had lost a great deal of weight on our voyage, and his veins looked like thick, angry cords beneath his skin. There were also sinister red streaks running up his arms and legs, and his face was grotesquely swollen. Freckles was concerned that he was suffering from severe blood poisoning. His own blood was killing him. No doubt he knew this himself, for he stood unsteadily in the boat one day, and looked at us with great gentleness and compassion.

'I'm going to have to leave you,' he quietly announced.

We looked at him, wondering what he could possibly mean. Our minds had slowed to the point where it took a while for things to register.

'I'm afraid that I simply cannot remain in the boat with you,' he continued. 'I'm a danger to you. I think it very likely that I will poison you all.'

Then he sat on the gunwale with his back to the Atlantic swell, and looked at each of us in turn with a serene smile.

'Goodbye.'

Before we had a chance to thank him for what he'd done for us, or say our own farewells, he allowed himself to topple backwards into the sea, the way scuba divers do. He disappeared.

We were utterly stunned by what that wonderful man had done. The enormity of his self-sacrifice was breathtaking, the nature of his goodness overwhelming. Freckles was the only one with the presence of mind to say exactly what needed to be said: 'Greater love hath no man than to lay down his life for his friends.'

There were so many dreadful moments in that boat, lots of them a blur even then, but the passing of Doctor Geoffrey Purslow was the worst. And his speech is stamped in my memory. Even today, more than 60 years later, I still weep for that brave and loving soul.

After the death of Purslow I thought I was done for. Up until then, despite the nightmare of our situation, I had clung to the hope that we'd be rescued. After all, we'd already seen one ship. Perhaps there would be others. But I slipped into despondency, my thoughts turning more and more to my family. *If I die and get lowered over the side, my body will never be found. How will they come to terms with the fact that I simply vanished?* They would have had no news of me since my time in Port Said. Those thoughts tore away at me and I suppose I was sinking into a deep depression. I would have given up completely had it not been for Freckles. She was a jolly, optimistic person and she pulled me out of my despair by talking about all kinds of everyday things. We'd have silly little conversations about food. It gave us something pleasant to think about.

'Jelly and custard. Now that would be nice, wouldn't it?'

'Not half as nice as a slice of roast beef.'

'With gravy.'

'That's right, lots and lots of gravy.'

Probably because we were English, the subject of drinking tea always seemed to come up, too.

'I fancy a nice cup of tea,' Freckles would say.

'So do I.'

'Milk and sugar?'

'Yes thanks.'

'Lovely.'

'I'd like a glass of cold water first, though.'

'Of course.'

Sometimes I'd tell her about the places I'd seen while serving on *Valiant*, about Bermuda and Halifax, Narvik and Gibraltar, Malta and Alexandria. I'd tell her about my time doing sentry duty on the quay at Port Said, the trip down the east coast of Africa escorting the Italian prisoners to Durban, and the peaceful days in the transit camp at Pietermaritzburg.

'We had the most beautiful milk in that camp,' I told her.

'Ah, wouldn't a glass of milk be just lovely?'

'Gallons and gallons of it, we had. It was the best milk in the world, that was. The farmers used to leave it outside our tents, and it was cold and creamy.'

I'm convinced those conversations kept me sane, although they weren't always cheerful. Freckles told me she happened to be aboard *Laconia* because a British couple in Africa had entrusted her to take their small infant back to Britain, where anxious relatives would be waiting.

'I lost my grip on the dear little soul as I was going over the side,' she said. She didn't elaborate, but her grief was palpable. 'I have to survive this, McLoughlin. If I don't, those poor people will never know how their beautiful child was lost.'

Her quiet determination to survive was clear to me. I thought if she could cope with all this tragedy, then so could I.

When I wasn't talking to Freckles I would wander into my own vague little world and drift from one surreal hallucination to another. In one of those tormenting episodes I saw myself die and move on to a weird afterlife in which small boats full of ghost-like people drifted about aimlessly in a bizarre, watery netherworld. In another one I travelled effortlessly back and forth through time and then, when my mind returned to the present I couldn't work out whether our lifeboat was something from the past or whether it belonged to the future.

The nearest I came to complete comprehension was late one afternoon, when I heard someone ask a question.

'What day is it?'

'It's October the second,' someone answered.

I vaguely recognised the date. October the second. I struggled with it for a little while and then connected it to the year. October the second, 1942.

'It's my birthday,' I announced. 'My twenty-first birthday.'

'Well, that calls for a celebration,' Freckles decided.

With that, the water ration was organised and when the familiar oblong tin was passed to me, there was more than my usual one tablespoon in the corner when I tilted it. It was a double ration for my birthday. A beautiful, sparkling, generous gift from a handful of people who needed it as much as I did, perhaps even more. That's how my 21st birthday was marked. It set me thinking. I forced myself to do the arithmetic. *Laconia* had been sunk on 12 September.

How long is that? It's the second of October now. Let me think ... hell, it's 20 days.

'We've been out here for twenty days,' I said to Freckles.

'Yes. I think that's right.'

'How long can we keep going?'

117

'A while yet,' she said with her usual encouraging smile, even though she knew that there was only a skerrick of water left in the tank.

With the realisation that we'd been drifting for three weeks, despair paid me another nasty visit. We were hopelessly lost, no one knew we were out here and there was no end in sight. I looked about me, at the deserted sea, at my deathly fellow survivors. There had been 68 of us in the beginning, and less than half of us were left. It was an unthinkable toll. And still people were dying every day.

When there were only about 20 of us left in the boat, those in the bow noticed a menacing restlessness among the small group gathered in the stern. A bullying attitude is what I'd call it. They were muttering about having a test, pulling an oar to prove we had a bit of strength left.

Will they throw me overboard if I don't measure up? Would they do it in the presence of the only woman left in the boat?

Huddled near this intimidating group was a sailor called Mickey. He was about the same age as me. One night there was a sudden commotion. Although it was dark, as usual I could still see ghostly outlines and vague shapes. There were agitated movements in the stern. Then I heard Mickey crying out.

'No, no, I can pull an oar!' There was panic in his voice.

I don't know why they picked on the poor chap. Perhaps it was simply because he happened to be near them, an easy target.

'I can row! I'm strong enough to pull an oar, please,' he pleaded. 'I don't want to go over!'

I heard the sounds of a struggle and more pleading

from Mickey. Then there was a splash and the commotion abruptly stopped. In its place came a chilling silence. I spent the rest of that night in a state of panic. *What's that noise? Is that person edging closer to me? What was that muffled conversation about? Have they decided I'm next, that someone else deserves my water ration more than me?*

Every little movement made me jump. I thought I was going mad. The night seemed to drag on forever. When the pale pink of dawn finally streaked the sky I looked around the boat carefully, half hoping that I had imagined the entire sordid episode. But Mickey wasn't with us anymore. I often hear that poor young sailor's desperate pleas when I can't find refuge in sleep, and I live through that cruel night all over again. The sheer ruthlessness shocks me still.

Only a day or two later we ran out of water and we all knew that we were finished, doomed to die of thirst in our horrible little boat, adrift God knows where in the vastness of the Atlantic.

And then it rained. It wasn't just the dampness of a drizzly sea fret, either. It was a roaring tropical downpour that lasted for several hours. Oddly, whenever I've recalled it, I've always seen it falling from a clear blue sky, but of course it couldn't have done. Freckles and a few others had been praying. Perhaps that tremendous rainstorm was the answer to their prayers. Miracle or not, the unexpected abundance of water when we were at our most desperate lifted our spirits instantly.

We ripped down our yellow canvas sail and, holding on to its three corners, used it to catch the cool, precious water.

It quickly turned yellow, but that didn't worry us in the least as we joyfully poured it from the canvas into the boat's water tank. It was absolutely beautiful, that water. We collected it in bailing tins, our empty biscuit tins, anything that would store some of it to drink later. And while we were busy collecting it we were totally drenched, standing there with our heads thrown back, mouths open to the sky, savouring it on swollen tongues and peeling, burnt faces, shouting and laughing and slapping each other on the back. We scooped up the water in our salt-caked hands and drank endless mouthfuls. Our fingers turned white and wrinkled and the temperature plummeted. We began shivering, but it was utterly marvellous because we had water.

When the rain finally stopped, we slid from sheer exhilaration to morbid sadness. With our searing thirst satisfied, and with water in the boat's tank once again, we realised that the rain was both sweet salvation and bitter tragedy. People had died under cruel circumstances in the days before because there wasn't enough water, and the remaining 16 of us were ankle deep in it.

The morning after our reprieve, however, it felt like nothing had changed. It was hotter than ever. Everything was dry again and our thirst returned with a vengeance. Although we had water, we knew there was little or no chance of rescue. This meant we had to preserve our new water supply just as carefully as we'd been doing all along. Our food rations were all but gone. A dreadful lethargy returned to the boat as we tried to keep cool beneath our makeshift shelter. The boat was silent, with just about everyone asleep. I felt light-headed and disorientated. The morning was eerily calm, the sea like a sheet of glinting glass. We had put the sail back up, but it was hanging limp. We were going nowhere. I started drifting in and out of sleep, unsure whether my dreams were reality or my reality a dream.

My family suddenly appeared and I was right there with them. It was teatime at home in Liverpool. We were sitting together around the kitchen table and my mother was heaping her delicious Irish stew onto our plates. Our usual Sunday treat, jelly and custard, was there on the table too. I was just about to take my first mouthful of the Irish stew when I woke up. I was completely overwhelmed by self-pity. *Why did I join the navy? I might have got married and had a family of my own and my wife would have made Irish stew and jelly and custard.* I knew I couldn't survive another day in that wretched boat. *I hope I die before I go mad.*

In the depths of misery and hopelessness, I lay in the bow next to Freckles and the young RAF chap. They were both half asleep, stupefied by the heat. I couldn't get comfortable, so I sat up and leant over the gunwale, chin on my hands, watching the water. One of our constant companions, a pilot fish, was swimming down there. I couldn't see him as clearly as I usually could and I wondered if my eyes were failing. Every other part of me certainly was. But I looked at the water again. It was brown.

I stared at the water a little longer, wondering what could have made it go from its usual clean green-blue to patches of cloudy brown. Then a dragonfly came into view, skimming across the surface of the water. Next I saw a butterfly. Then some fragments of vegetation drifted past, bits of twigs and leaves. I forced my head up and tried to focus on the horizon. All I could see were a couple of dots.

Christ, I'm going blind.

I watched the dots until more of them appeared. My heart began to thump. I quietly nudged the RAF chap awake and, without saying anything, pointed to the horizon. From the look on his face I knew I wasn't going mad or blind. I shook Doris.

'Freckles,' I whispered. 'Look, can you see what I can see? It's a convoy of ships.'

Drowsy and confused, my dear companion raised herself and looked over the gunwale.

'Yes, I see it,' she said.

'It's a convoy, I'm sure it is.'

'Don't say anything to the others just yet. Wait a bit. We must be sure before we tell them,' Freckles said. Despite everything she had been through, she still had the presence of mind not to raise hope in the others. It would be too much for everyone to bear if it turned out to be a mirage.

So the three of us waited and watched, perplexed. The dots didn't seem to be moving. But they kept getting bigger until they appeared more like smudges. Then, ever so gradually, sticks appeared on top of them.

'Those are ships' masts, those are,' I said.

'We'll wait a bit more, McLoughlin.'

The tension was unbearable.

'Oh, my God,' I said. 'They're not masts, they're trees. It's land!' I looked at Freckles. There were tears in her eyes. 'That's why the water's gone brown, we're near land!'

We shook the others awake.

9

The pain of survival

My spirits soared from rock bottom to the greatest exal-tation I've ever experienced. I'll never forget that over-whelming relief. I hoped like hell it wasn't just another lapse into my half-world of hallucination. We were 16 human wrecks who'd been resigned to die in our dreadful boat, gaping at the land we'd been faithfully steering toward for a month.

'Dear Lord, we're there.'

'Where are we, do you think?'

'Africa. It must be Africa.'

'We'll be all right now.'

We were like children on a long-awaited outing, laughing, offering opinions. We allowed ourselves an extra ration of water to celebrate. Perhaps it was the knowledge that fresh water must certainly be near that made our extra ration taste so ghastly, even though it was welcome.

'The water's gone off.'

'How long to get ashore?'

'Couple of hours.'

'More like another day. It's not as close as it looks.'

'Bollocks to that. I'm not spending another bloody day in this boat.'

So we made one last attempt to row. But we were too

weak. And there was little wind, so we had to sit it out and let nature take its course. That was sheer hell, seeing land right in front of us and not being able to reach it. And all the time, as we stared and waited, the land drew closer. By late afternoon we could see green hills and palm trees. They looked so exotic it was breathtaking. Seabirds wheeled and squawked overhead.

'The air smells different,' someone observed.

'That's what land smells like.'

The heady, sweet scent of tropical vegetation was intoxicating and frustrating.

'We're not going to drift that far before dark,' I said.

'Yes we will,' the RAF chap answered.

The sun went down and blotted out our gorgeous view of palm trees and green hills, toying painfully with our hope. Of all the long nights we'd spent in that God-forsaken boat, that was certainly the longest. No one slept. We were too keyed up, talking about what the next morning might bring.

During the night we drifted a little closer to shore, but not nearly close enough for our liking. At dawn, the land was right there in full and tantalising view again, yet it still remained beyond our grasp.

During the afternoon a four-engine flying boat appeared. Many of us wept as it banked and swept around us in a bellowing turn, its wingtip floats just above the water. It was all brilliant silver in the morning sun, and when we saw the Union Jack painted on its fuselage we knew that we were going to be rescued. It was just a matter of how.

Frail and unsteady as we were, all of us managed to stand

up and wave as that majestic machine circled. A figure waved back from one of its windows. Someone grabbed the board with *SOS Water* marked on it in white lead. Tragically, *Laconia*'s engineer and bosun were no longer with us to help hold up their sign. The flying boat headed briefly for the land before returning to roar past us like it was on a bombing run. A lifejacket wrapped around a big linen bag like a pillowcase dropped from its hull and splashed into the water just a few yards from our boat. It was a fantastic shot! Unfortunately, the bag broke open as it struck the water, scattering its contents of apples, tomatoes and pears. The wind was up again and the precious fruit bobbed away from us on the choppy waves.

One of the group from the stern dived over the side, retrieved the bag and two or three pieces of fruit, then swam back to us. When he hauled himself over the gunwale and back into the boat, I was suspicious of his unexpected display of strength after everything we'd been through. Freckles was quick to echo my concern.

'Goodness, how did he have the strength to do that?' she asked.

I do believe people played God in that boat. But my doubts were quickly swept aside when someone found a note inside the bag and read it aloud:

Okay, help coming. You are 60 miles south of Monrovia.

'Anyone know where Monrovia is?'

'Isn't that in Europe?'

'Doesn't sound very African. Perhaps this isn't the African coast after all.'

'This is Africa all right.'

But it wasn't important. All we cared about was that help was coming. That flying boat was a Godsend, it really was. It thundered over us several more times, then flew off and disappeared, leaving us to drift and wonder aloud.

'Why didn't they just set down on the water?'

'Too choppy.'

'Who do you think will come and rescue us?'

'A British ship I should think.'

'I don't want to be on no more bleedin' ships,' a sailor said.

'Me either,' I agreed with feeling.

'If the sea calms down later on, the flying boat might come back.'

'That would be something. Imagine flying away from here on that beautiful aeroplane!'

By mid-afternoon we could see waves crashing against rocks, sending plumes of white spray into the air and booming in the distance. It didn't look too safe to me.

'That's no place for a small boat in among that lot. Getting in there's going to be tricky,' I said to another navy bloke. But something had caught his eye.

'I think there's a beach,' he said. 'See? There's one spot where there's no spray. That means no rocks.'

He was right. There was a small white beach between the rocks and a jungle-covered headland. But the breeze swung around to blow offshore and we drifted out to sea again. Our fragile morale crumbled when the sound of the surf disappeared along with our beach and people began cursing. The sea was reluctant to set us free.

The offshore breeze tormented us for most of the afternoon, and then swung around to blow us back in again.

The light was fading and the wind was really stirring up the waves. The boat moved steadily toward the shoreline, the booming of the surf increased and spumes were being flung up by the rocks like white beacons in the gathering darkness. That spray got me very edgy. Then a large wave reared up behind us and we weren't in a lifeboat anymore, we were in a surfboat! We were really moving. It was all very nerve-wracking, what with the looming darkness, the boat lurching on the big roller beneath us, and the booming of the surf ahead. Everyone was hanging on for dear life. But the sailor at the tiller skillfully kept us pointing at the beach.

'We're going in!

'Don't let it broach!'

Apart from hitting the rocks, broaching was my biggest fear. I had a fleeting vision of us all drowning a few yards from salvation. Then, right underneath my feet, the bow struck sand and another wave caught up with us to slew the boat sideways. The chap at the tiller lost control and the boat pitched upwards and then rolled violently onto its side. We were catapulted into the shallows where the waves were crashing onto the beach. It was mayhem. We were a cursing heap of humanity, tossed out like so much garbage on a tropical beach in the middle of nowhere. Most of us pulled ourselves through the wet sand on our stomachs, just like in the movies. One or two tried to stand up, but tottered about wildly before collapsing into the waves again. We were completely done in. I crawled until I finally felt the sand go dry, and I gave up. I couldn't move another inch.

'Everyone all right?'

'I don't believe it. We made it.'

We lay there for ages in the darkness, trying to comprehend that we were actually on land. My bitten leg was throbbing so badly it felt as if it was going to burst open. I had putrid sores and weeping boils all over me and they were full of coarse sand and shell grit. Even the slightest movement felt like someone was attacking my open wounds with sandpaper. Everyone was moaning and groaning and shivering. I attempted to stand up, pushing myself slowly onto my feet. After almost a month at sea, the beach felt as though it heaved beneath me and I promptly fell like a sack of potatoes. I couldn't even take a single step.

Gradually we gathered our wits. A few people went back to the boat, which was wallowing on its side in the shallows. They retrieved various bits and pieces, clothes and tins, things like that, and some of our remaining water. Then we decided to stay on the beach until morning, which suited me fine because I knew I couldn't move. I couldn't even crawl. So we huddled together for security, knowing we had survived the sea but unsure if we were really safe. The surf boomed in front of us while God knows what lurked in the jungle behind us. I think a few people were already asleep sitting up.

'What's that?' an anxious voice suddenly whispered.

'Where?'

'I saw a light.'

That really got our nerves going, but soon we could all see it, a lantern light swinging and swaying along the beach toward us. I can still picture that light and how my imagination ran off into terrifying thoughts of wild savages hunting us down. People of my generation grew up believing there were still cannibals in Africa. Then we heard voices speaking a language we didn't recognise and our desperate band huddled closer together with growing apprehension.

'What's going to happen here?' I muttered to Freckles.

'They're natives, look,' she said.

The mysterious group approached and formed a half-circle around us, chattering away to one another and pointing at us in the glaring yellow light of their lantern. They were an imposing bunch, all bulky, muscle-bound Negro men, quite short and stocky with deep brown skin that looked like it had been polished. A few of them had white paint or tattoos on their faces and arms. They were dressed in odd scraps of clothing, a torn shirt here, threadbare trousers there. Some were bare-chested with colourful sarongs wrapped around their lower bodies. One man had an ancient peaked cap perched on his round head. We quickly realised that he was their leader. We could understand a little of what he was saying, with scraps of English all muddled up with his own language.

Behind him, others were jabbering away and laughing and giggling among themselves, seemingly with relief.

'We cry,' the big leader bloke said to us. 'Watch you longa time on water, not reach poor people. Two days cry for you in village.'

Then there was a hell of a racket as they performed a wild, uninhibited dance in the eerie lantern light on the beach, with our ramshackle boat floundering in the surf behind them. And while they rejoiced around us, we simply

sat on the sand and cried our hearts out. It really hit us
that we had survived and we were just swamped by a boiling
mix of relief, happiness, terrible sadness, pain and illness.
A dam wall seemed to have burst inside us. In between
our gut-wrenching sobs we drew breath and laughed, then
went back to our sobbing.

When we settled down, someone asked where we were.
The leader chap told us we were in West Africa.

'Liberia,' he said. 'This place, Liberia.'

Liberia. Well, bloody hell. What about that, then?

We really had made it to Africa. Werner Hartenstein
didn't think we would make it, but we'd rowed, sailed and
drifted 700 miles in an open boat.

The leader gave instructions to his men, and one of
them approached me with a big grin. Without so much
as a word, he slung me over his shoulder as if I was an
empty sack. To him I probably was. There wasn't much
left of me, just skin and bone. From his shoulder I noticed
the men were in awe of Freckles.

Maybe they've never seen a white woman before.

One of them approached her with what almost amounted
to reverence, stooping down to piggyback her effortlessly.
She too was utterly wasted away.

'Stay with white mammy,' I instructed my chap.

'White mammy, white mammy,' Freckles' man echoed.
Maybe he thought I was her husband or something, I'm
not sure, but he got a good grip on her.

'Walk bare feet very bad,' the boss man told us. 'Worms
get inside feet for very bad trouble.'

This seemed odd because he and his band were barefoot, but we gathered there were parasites in the soil that would invade any splits or sores in the soles of our feet. Many of us had been barefoot throughout the voyage and our feet were in a very bad state, so I was pretty pleased to be hanging over the shoulders of one of those burly blokes. Others who were too weak to walk also got picked up and carried. Those who still wore the remnants of their shoes and socks hobbled along on weakened, unsteady legs.

The boss led the way from the beach, holding up his lantern as he followed a narrow path through the jungle. All I could see was the strong, confident feet of the bloke carrying me, but I felt damp jungle foliage brushing against my head and feet. I could hear the strident chirping of crickets or cicadas. And the crashing surf faded until there was just the excited chatter of the Negroes and the groans of their exhausted cargo. We went through the jungle for what seemed a long time. The humidity was stifling away from the coast.

Then we emerged from the narrow jungle path into an African village that looked for all the world like the set from one of those old Saturday matinee Tarzan adventures. When I lifted my head I felt certain I had died and moved on to another world, a strange new place where I would start my life again as someone else. There was an open square and a number of small straw huts arranged in a semi-circle, with cooking fires and tall flame sticks burning in front of them. Pungent wood smoke hung in the heavy, humid air. Shy women and children emerged from the darkness to watch our pathetic little procession stagger into their lives.

Our rescuers carried us to a raised platform in a huge communal shelter at the centre of the village square. It had a straw roof but no walls, I guess for ventilation in the suffocating heat. We just collapsed there, a heap of spent humanity, some of us barely conscious. A crowd of villagers gathered around to stare at us. We must have looked ghastly in the flickering light of their flame sticks. We were wet from the surf, caked in salt and covered in sores. We were as alien to them as they were to us. The women had colourful designs painted on their bodies. I was ignorant of other cultures then, and felt a little intimidated, unsure of what they had in mind.

Those people were absolutely marvellous to us. After they had satisfied their initial curiosity, they brought us all kinds of fruit and some coconut milk. I couldn't face any of it. My body, I'm sure, was very close to packing up completely. It had grown accustomed to not having food and was feeding on itself, eating the life out of me from the inside. I drank a few mouthfuls of the water from the lifeboat, nothing more. I don't think anyone else ate or drank much, either. Our tongues were too swollen and our mouths too sore to chew on anything.

Everything was a blur after that. I half heard a few of our group talking with the head man, but I couldn't make any sense of it. And a deafening downpour set in, which only added to my confusion. It absolutely belted down and poured off the hut's straw roof like a waterfall. Instead of cooling the air down, though, it seemed to get hotter and stickier, making it hard to breath. Then swarms of mosquitoes attacked us. Their bites were ferocious and unrelenting. I just lay on that platform listening to the rain and little scraps of meaningless conversation. Then I sank into a deep, black void, the sleep of the near-dead.

The next morning was like waking up in some extra-ordinary lost age, a forgotten time from another century. Strangely, it was the quietness that woke me. The village seemed to be holding its breath. There was no sound, no movement. For a month the mournful sound of Atlantic waves against the hull of our wooden boat had been the background to our misery, and the sudden absence of sound and motion made me feel uneasy and off balance. The sensation gradually passed as the village stirred and, although it all seemed unreal, it was extremely beautiful to watch.

It got light very slowly because the sky was like lead, still swollen with dark, brooding rain clouds. I smiled when a cockerel crowed; we were part of civilisation again. The war and all its horror seemed remote and the utter simplicity of the timeless place was extremely pleasant. Dogs emerged to sniff and scratch their way around the village. People came out of the smaller huts to light cooking fires. Except for small children with swollen bellies, who peered at us from a little way off, the villagers no longer payed attention to the sorry collection of survivors in their communal hut. The smell of damp wood burning reached me through the open sides of the long hut, mixing with the rich scent of steaming tropical vegetation. And soon I could smell food cooking, but there were still no stirrings of hunger inside me.

Then my mind slipped out of gear and a dreamy, soothing

peace came over me. I was aware of plans being made around me, of people talking and moving about, but I was unable to participate. It was more than just a vague detachment. I was in another place altogether. I've read descriptions of so-called out-of-body experiences, and it was a little like that in some ways. There was a peculiar sense of being there while seeing and hearing everything from afar. I wasn't hallucinating like I had in the boat, but I was certainly adrift. I could feel, yet was numb at the same time.

I heard little snatches of the conversation between the village headman and a few of our group, something about a trading post further along the coast. A name, Grand Bassa, was repeated a number of times. Then a group of Negro men led a few of the more able survivors out of the village. The rest of us watched them go from our positions on the platform.

'Are you all right?' Freckles asked me. I couldn't answer.

Later, in the afternoon, a native runner brought a letter to the headman, who then came and talked to us in a very excited way.

'Boats coming from Bassa,' I heard him say.

I had no idea what this meant, so I continued to lie there while a flurry of activity started up around me. Our group was getting up, collecting meagre possessions and preparing themselves to move on. I couldn't work out why they would want to do that. I just watched them. I must have seemed totally useless. Well, I was. Then one of the village men came to me and, smiling all the time, gently helped me to my feet. He knew I couldn't walk so he hoisted me onto his back. Another man stooped to carry Freckles piggyback.

They took us back to the beach where we'd landed the night before. Our boat was still there, tipped on its side with the surf rolling in against the peeling grey paint and filthy weed and barnacles that encrusted the hull. It was a shambles, and very sad to see. I had no great affection for it, but it had seen us safely to Africa.

We sat on the beach for what seemed like ages. Then a fleet of native outrigger canoes came gliding along the coast. They had tall, majestic sails that made me wonder if I was in some kind of nautical heaven. When the chap who had carried me to the beach picked me up again and waded powerfully into the water toward them, it finally sank in that those big canoes had come to collect us. I didn't want to get in an open boat again, but it was completely out of my hands.

I was lifted into one of the canoes and sat facing the stern as several Negro crewmen mucked about with the giant sail towering over me. There was a lot of singing and shouting and good humour, like they were making a festive occasion of it. I didn't feel too festive, though. Being in that canoe brought old fears rushing back, and I started panicking. The hull was nothing more than a hollowed-out tree trunk with curved branches for outriggers. It was just wide enough for one person to sit between the gunwales and it rode so low that water was slopping in over the sides.

I don't want to be here.

In the middle of the canoe was a huge cooking pot with a fire burning on the rough-hewn timber hull beneath it.

Those chaps were cooking a meal in the middle of their canoe. My mind slipped a little more out of gear. Whenever I think of it, I only see those powerful black crewmen, the massive sail overhead, the cooking pot over the open fire, and me sitting there unable to make sense of any of it.

The crew got the sail up and, together with the other canoes carrying my fellow-survivors, we raced along the coast, cutting through the water as smoothly as any boat I'd ever been on. It would have been exhilarating if I hadn't been so out of it, but it just frightened the life out of me. To take my mind off the water, rushing by six inches either side of me, I kept my eyes on the cooking pot. I was fascinated by it. *How the hell did they get that bloody great thing in the boat?* If someone had told me of such a thing I would never have believed it.

Several hours later we sailed into Grand Bassa. It was only a tiny coastal settlement, a minor trading post, but it seemed big to me after being in the jungle village; there were real houses scattered about. A crowd, perhaps the entire population, had gathered on the beach to greet us and help us ashore. The other few survivors who had left the village earlier in the day were there. There were women in beautiful white dresses and tall, dignified men in immaculate linen shirts, shorts and pith helmets. They were mostly Dutch, but there were a few Syrians as well, yet they all spoke perfect English.

Some of the women were crying in sympathy because of our terrible condition. They were aghast at the sight of us. We must have looked like the walking dead. I knew that they would be able to look after us properly, perhaps give us badly needed medical treatment. I started to cry and it was a long time before I stopped. Over the following days and weeks I would often find myself crying. I couldn't control it and, in my general confusion, I wondered what was wrong with me.

10

Freetown farewell

The healing process began for us in Bassa. Well, the physical healing at least. We were billeted in various houses around the settlement. I went with Freckles and a couple of air force chaps to a home shared by two incredibly kind Dutchmen. One of the first things they did was give me a bath. I was disgusting, covered in salt, oil, weeping sores and deep, putrid ulcers that looked like miniature volcano craters. I'll never forget the soap. It wasn't soft, creamy soap. It was hard, like pumice, and just about scraped off what little flesh still clung to me. It was like rubbing stone on bone. That's all I was by that stage, bone. They got me cleaned up pretty well, though, and gave me a shave, too. It was luxury. They fitted us out with clothes donated by different people in the settlement. The generosity we found in Bassa touched us all deeply.

We were given beds with clean linen in bright, airy rooms, and I spent days in bed, a mosquito net over me, relishing the feeling of safety. And slowly, very slowly, I began to eat again. Freckles put us all on a diet of Quaker Oats, milk and fruit. It was difficult to keep down at first but gradually we began to feel hungry and could eat more and more. We steadily gained strength and started moving about without too much trouble. I put on a bit of weight, but I've never been as big and strong as I was before the sinking.

The Dutch brought us medicine and wonderfully soothing ointments for our sores. But they arrived too late for one of us, a soldier, who fell seriously ill when a septic sore on his leg refused to heal. He was in agony and soon developed a raging fever. His face was so swollen he couldn't speak. A Liberian doctor came to the settlement and arranged for him to be taken to Freetown, the coastal capital of Sierra Leone. A few days later the poor man died of gas gangrene. It was tragic, after all he had endured. So, in the end, only 15 of us survived.

Thankfully, I improved physically, but my mind was still in a bad way. I couldn't concentrate on anything for more than a few seconds. We sat around together in our billet playing Ludo and draughts, but I was hopelessly lost with those games, even though they'd been such a familiar part of my childhood. There were books, too, but I had to read a sentence again and again to work out what it meant. So I mostly spent my time lying about, my mind drifting. Once I'd found my feet I took short, aimless walks around the settlement, only half aware of where I was.

I felt utterly lost. I knew I was safe, I knew I wanted to go home, but I had no idea how I was going to get there. I was in limbo, waiting for something to happen, waiting for others to decide what to do with me. Time still held no meaning. I now know that we were in Bassa for 11 days. We had been torpedoed on 12 September and spent 28 days in the lifeboat, so it was well past the middle of October when we were recovering in Grand Bassa. During our time there a message was sent to the British chargé d'affaires in Monrovia, explaining our presence. He eventually sent a ship from Freetown to pick us up.

That ship was HMS *Spaniard*, a naval support trawler. She was the most rundown ship I'd ever seen, a rust bucket with a pretty rough crew. She anchored a little way off shore and sent her boat to pick us up. When I climbed aboard *Spaniard* it was immediately obvious that I was back in the navy.

'Name?' an officer asked.

'Able Seaman McLoughlin, sir.'

'Last ship?'

'*Valiant*, but I was torpedoed on *Laconia*,' I told him.

'Very good. Go below, get your rum issue.'

'Aye aye, sir.'

I went below and they tried to get me to drink some rum, but the thought of it made my stomach heave. A navy man had to be pretty sick if he didn't want his rum! Even though the crew was a rough bunch, they were sympathetic and left me alone. *Spaniard* was a weary old ship. She crawled along for two days and nights before a frigate drew alongside and both vessels stopped dead in the water. We were transferred to the frigate. We hadn't been aboard for more than a few hours, steaming full-ahead for Freetown, when a submarine alert was sounded on the ship's klaxon. There was a frantic rush to action stations. I had nothing to do because I wasn't part of the crew. I was supposed to go below but there was absolutely no way I was going to do that with a submarine lurking about. If a torpedo hit, I wanted to be up top and ready for a quick escape. So I stayed on deck and watched as the crew set a string of depth charges over the side. Every nerve in my body was on full alert. I was unravelling again.

When we got to Freetown the various military commands and civilian authorities made different arrangements for us, and our little party of survivors broke up. We went our separate ways without any emotion at all. There was no sadness or ceremony. After everything we'd been through together, our farewells were strangely matter-of-fact.

'Cheerio then, McLoughlin,' Freckles said.

'Bye Freckles. Thanks for everything.'

'We won't forget our little journey in a hurry,' she said. At the time I didn't appreciate the magnitude of her understatement.

'No.'

'Good luck.'

'And good luck to you.'

There were no promises of meeting again, no exchanges of addresses. There was a war on, and we all simply had to get on with it. What had happened to us was, after all, just one tiny wave in the massive tide of a world conflict. So we just said goodbye and that was it.

There was a Royal Navy hospital ship moored in Freetown harbour, the *Edinburgh Castle*. She was a big, white vessel with red crosses on her hull. I was taken on board along with Gibson, the sailor who had pulled me aboard the lifeboat all those weeks ago. The medical staff gave us a thorough physical examination with great compassion and kindness, and told me I was suffering from malnutrition. I could have told them that. They appeared overly concerned about the festering sores that were still plaguing me.

'We need to get those fixed up,' one of the doctors told me. 'We'll dress them with lint bandages soaked in salt water.'

When I laughed at that he seemed slightly annoyed. But in my mind it was the constant exposure to salt water that had got those sores started in the first place.

'Well, you know best doctor,' I said, and left it at that.

A day or so later some officers came aboard the hospital ship to debrief Gibson and me about the sinking of *Laconia*. When I told them I'd been aboard U-156 they got quite excited, urging me to give them details of the submarine's control room, but all I could remember with any clarity was that the diesel engines were made in Augsburg.

While I waited impatiently for my sores to heal I made friends with the medical staff on the *Edinburgh Castle*. After a few days they suggested going ashore to have a look around Freetown.

'Come on, Mac. Let's try some of the local food.'

I was keen for any distraction, so we wandered aimlessly for a while, taking in the sights until we came across a dilapidated little shack that served meals. We decided on chicken, and knew it was going to be fresh when we saw a huge Negro woman chasing a chicken around the ramshackle yard within sight of our table. She caught the frantically flapping creature by the legs and lopped its head off with a machete right in front of us. This didn't help my already meagre appetite. But she cooked it for us straight away and what little I could eat was very tasty indeed.

Word came while I was resting aboard the *Edinburgh*

Castle that I was being drafted to HMS *Hecla*, a destroyer depot ship berthed near us in the harbour. She was going to England. *With any sort of luck, I might be home for Christmas.* I could barely imagine it, seeing my family again, being surrounded once more by people who loved me. I couldn't wait to leave the oppressive heat and humidity of West Africa. However, within hours of receiving this wonderful news, terrible shivering tremors gripped my entire body. I felt as if I'd been thrust into a freezer, yet sweat poured out of me in torrents. A headache hammered at my temples, my joints became so painful I wanted to scream, and what little energy I had drained out of me. My temperature was 105 and I was delirious with fever. A distant and distorted voice said something about malaria.

The shivers and shakes stayed with me for many days, racking my body for hours at a time and then disappearing, leaving me in a tangle of soggy sheets, totally spent and dehydrated. In those peaceful hours, my mind drifted back to the mosquitoes that had attacked us so viciously while we lay in the big hut in the village. Then the symptoms started all over again. The high fever raged and I was urged to drink what seemed like gallons of water until the crisis finally passed. But it left me as limp as a wet rag, seriously setting back my recovery. I was pretty frail.

'You might have attacks like that on and off for years,' the doctor said. I must have looked horrified because he patted me on the shoulder sympathetically. 'That's how it is with malaria, unfortunately.'

While I was delirious, HMS *Hecla* left Freetown harbour without me. I was devastated when I found out. But a few days later, I was lying about in a dark frame of mind when the doctor came to see me.

'How are you feeling?' he asked.

'Pretty awful. I was supposed to be going home on *Hecla*.'

'I know how disappointed you must be.'

'Yes,' I said. 'My bad luck, I guess.'

'It was your very good luck I'd say. She's been sunk. Torpedoed.' I went numb. 'A U-boat hit her west of the Straits of Gibraltar. There's been a huge loss of life,' the doctor said.

That terrible news hit me hard. I'd been drafted to two ships that had been torpedoed after circumstances denied me a chance to join them. I'd been aboard a torpedoed ship and survived. I'd been aboard a German U-boat while it was bombed and survived. I'd been adrift in a lifeboat in the Atlantic for 28 days and survived.

What the hell does all this mean? What's my life all about? How did I survive when I should, by rights, be dead? Am I just lucky or is there something guiding me through all this chaos?

I had no answers, but the first tiny seeds of my faith were planted as I lay in that hospital ship in Freetown.

11

The hard way home

Once I had more or less got over the malaria they drafted me
to HMS *Dragon*, a very old cruiser. She was in Freetown, preparing to sail for Britain where she would be decommissioned.

'You'll sign on as crew,' I was told bluntly.

I was still desperately ill and hopelessly detached, so
the prospect of hard physical work was daunting. *Oh well,
at least I'm going home!* No one seemed to care that I was
just out of hospital after suffering from malnutrition and
malaria. I was a wreck, but there were no free rides and
little compassion. So, around the middle of November,
I went aboard *Dragon*. I was kitted out in a replacement
uniform that hung limply from my scarecrow frame, anxious
to be on my way. A few hours out of Freetown I was on
deck when the division officer approached me.

'What was your last ship?' he asked me.

'*Valiant*, sir.'

'What was your job?'

'Gun crew.'

'We'll make you a lookout, then.'

The logic of that escaped me.

'Where, sir?'

'Up there,' he said, pointing to the crow's nest at the
top of *Dragon*'s main mast.

'Aye aye, sir.'

There was no point in arguing or trying to explain, surrounded by a battle-hardened crew, that I was too weak to do it. They had all experienced plenty of unpleasant things, so I knew I couldn't expect any favours. It was something to be accepted without complaint.

So I climbed with my weak legs shaking until I reached the yardarm near the top of the 80-foot mast. The crow's nest perched on the yardarm was like an over-sized metal bucket, with just enough room for one man and a telephone. It was impossible to sit down. When I reached the top I had to stretch out onto the yardarm to make room for the other sailor on the masthead watch to get out of the crow's nest. Then I climbed in to start my two-hour watch.

It was a spectacular vantage point. When I looked straight down, the guns on the foredeck appeared no bigger than my fingers, and the sailors moving about on the deck where just tiny uniformed figures. The view of the bow cleaving its path through the sea was impressive. From that lofty perch the ocean appeared so vast that it was easy to believe I'd never see land again, that the world was nothing but green sea and whitecaps.

The weather was cool as we steered into the North Atlantic, and we soon struck rough seas. It was a wild ride on top of that mast, like swinging on a giant upside-down pendulum, but I managed to spend most of my watch peering anxiously through a pair of binoculars. My job was to report any ship sightings to the bridge. I was terrified of U-boats, of course, and it took a lot of concentration to distinguish between what I was seeing through the binoculars and what was raging through my imagination. Any disturbance on the surface was a periscope as far as I was concerned. My nerves were really jangling.

Just south of the Azores, I was on duty in the crow's nest when I sensed that *Dragon* was slowing. The bow wave got smaller and smaller until it disappeared altogether and the old cruiser stopped. My telephone rang. It was the officer of the watch telling me that there was a problem with the engines.

'Keep a sharp lookout,' he said.

'Aye aye, sir.'

He didn't have to remind me. I knew only too well that a cruiser dead in the water was a sitting duck for a U-boat commander. My imagination went into top gear.

Maybe Hartenstein is out here somewhere. He could be looking at us right now, his crew setting the ranges on their torpedoes.

But I figured the crow's nest was safer than being at action stations below deck somewhere. If *Dragon* was torpedoed and rolled over, I thought I'd be able to ride the mast all the way down to the water.

It took several hours to get the engines running again and then we got slowly underway, steering for the Azores. When we arrived, *Dragon* berthed in a pokey little harbour on a rocky island while more work was done on the engines.

The Azores, of course, were Portuguese and therefore neutral territory. The Portuguese wharf labourers told us very proudly that there was a German U-boat berthed just around the corner from us. I was horrified. The U-boat was the buzz throughout the ship within minutes. Everyone was keen to go and have a look at it.

'Coming to see the U-boat, Mac?' a sailor in my mess asked.

'I know what a U-boat looks like,' I said. He glanced sideways at me, a bit put out.

'Suit yourself. Once in a lifetime chance, though.'

I didn't try to explain. He probably wouldn't have believed me anyway. The word came back that the U-boat was holed up in the Azores for the same reason as *Dragon*. I was astonished and didn't like it one little bit. There was nothing to stop it signalling our presence, or leaving harbour before us and lying in wait.

But the U-boat was still there as we pulled out of harbour a few days later. I went back on duty in the crow's nest and was even more vigilant than before. However, apart from the weather becoming foul, nothing happened. As we ploughed through increasingly severe storms, I decided the Irish certainly knew a thing or two when they called the Atlantic 'the sea of bitter tears'. I just about froze to death on the masthead. Climbing down with numb hands and feet was pretty dicey. It was best not to think of the consequences of falling.

Eventually, after many days of pounding through heavy seas, *Dragon* approached England. When I heard we were going to dock in Liverpool I was absolutely ecstatic! After all this time, the Royal Navy was going to deliver me virtually to my front doorstep. We sailed through St George's Channel into the Irish Sea, skirted around Anglesey and finally into Liverpool Bay.

The morning we glided up the River Mersey is etched forever in my memory. I was off watch, so I went to the upper deck to savour the moment. It was a brilliantly sharp winter's day, absolutely beautiful with a miraculous blue sky, a few puffy white clouds hovering about. The Mersey was like glass below me as we slipped past Liverpool's famous light ship, anchored at the river mouth to warn ships of the sandbar there. My nostrils filled with the salt-and-tar smells of my childhood and, when we steered for Gladstone Dock, I was swamped by emotion. I'd come full circle. Gladstone Dock was where, in 1938, I had gone aboard the battleship *Royal Oak* and decided to join the Royal Navy. Four years later I was back in the very same place. But I wasn't the same person.

Dragon had barely tied up when gangs of dock workers rushed aboard to start the job of decommissioning her. After I'd completed my duties, which took me through to the afternoon, I was assigned to the shore watch, so I was free to leave the ship. I was off her like a shot, although I had to be back the next morning. I must have looked a sight in my baggy uniform, thin as a bean pole, clutching a battered little suitcase I'd scrounged.

I had a fair way to go. While I was serving in the Mediterranean, my parents had written to say they'd moved from my boyhood home in Walton, to Speke, near Liverpool Airport. So first I caught a train on the overhead railway to Pier Head, where I could catch a bus. I waited for a short time at the bus stop, pent up with emotion at the prospect of seeing my family again, and eventually a green bus rumbled along. I climbed onto its rear platform where a very big woman in an even bigger conductor's uniform blocked my way. I smiled at her but she didn't smile back.

'Where are you going, Jack?' she demanded.

'Home, to Speke. Out near the airport.'

'Well, you're not going there on this bus.'

'What?'

'You're not going to Speke or nowhere else on this bus.'

'Why not?'

'It's for war workers only, this bus, that's why not.'

I was absolutely dumbfounded. Unknown to me, special buses were allocated to factory workers directly involved in the war effort. Here I was, in the uniform of the Royal Navy, being barred from travelling on one of them. What sort of work did she think the navy did?

'But . . .'

'On your way, Jack. War workers only on this bus.'

She was such an imposing, intimidating woman that I meekly did as she said, and the bus drove off with her standing impassively on the back, a cold statue of authority. It was the last straw. Stranded there at the bus stop in the middle of town, clutching my suitcase, I felt like the most pathetic human specimen of all time. And just to complete the picture I had one of my all-too-frequent crying spells. The frustration was overwhelming. What a welcome home.

War workers be damned!

It got dark. I waited over an hour before getting on another bus that took me out to Speke. I got off and found 9 Hale Road, the family home I'd never seen. It was right next door to a church. I didn't have a key, of course, so I knocked on the front door.

For years afterwards my three sisters, Florence, Dorothy

and Enid would argue good-naturedly over who actually opened the door that night. I certainly don't know because I was engulfed in the most wonderful emotional chaos. All I remember was being swamped by them, wrapped in their arms, the three of them almost collapsing with the shock of seeing me. They looked at me in total disbelief, saying my name over and over, tears streaming down their faces.

'Oh God, Jim, we thought you were dead!'

'A letter came from the Admiralty.'

'Lost at sea, it said.'

'No one told us you were safe.'

'We didn't know.'

'Where are Mum and Dad?' I managed to ask through it all.

'They went out, to see a film. They're at the cinema.'

'Is it really you? You're so thin.'

'It's me, all right,' I said.

One of the girls ran out and went to a neighbour's place to ask if they could go and get my mother and father. When they eventually came home there was another torrent of tears, disbelief and shock.

'Jim, dear, what have they done to you?' my mother asked, her voice trembling.

Did we have a time that night! My brother George wasn't there because he was serving in the Fleet Air Arm, but the rest of us celebrated my return until I was dead on my feet, unable to speak or cry anymore.

Someone must have put me to bed.

12

Adrift on land

The next morning I awoke late. In fact extremely late, well past the time I was due to report back to the ship. I groaned and got moving. Within a few minutes I was in my uniform and heading for the front door.

'Cup of tea, Jim?' my mother asked. She and the others had been up for ages. In all the excitement of my home-coming I'd completely forgotten to mention that I still had duties on the ship, so they had innocently let me sleep in.

'Can't. I have to report back to *Dragon*.'

'That doesn't seem fair,' she said. 'You've only been home one night.'

'It's the navy, Mum. Don't worry, I'll be getting some Christmas leave soon.'

I said hurried goodbyes and made my way to the docks, knowing I would be in trouble the moment I went up the gangplank in full view of the crew on duty. But I had to face the music, which came soon enough and loud enough. There was an RPO, a regulation petty officer, on deck as I came aboard. He wasn't smiling.

'You're late, Able Seaman.'

'Yes, sir. Slept in, sir.'

'Name?'

'McLoughlin, sir.'

'What do you mean you slept in?'

'Well, I was pretty tired, sir.' The simple truth of it even sounded pathetic to me.

'What sort of excuse is that? We're all bloody well tired!'

'Sir.'

'Commander's Report!' he bellowed at me.

'Aye aye, sir.'

Any seaman getting back late to his ship was labelled a defaulter, pure and simple, and I had to face the wrath of the executive officer, under the pitiless eye of the RPO. I lined up with a number of other defaulters to discover my punishment.

'Caps off!' the RPO ordered.

'Name?' the Executive Officer asked without looking up from the papers on his desk.

'Able Seaman McLoughlin, sir.'

'Charge?'

'Late back to the ship, sir,' the RPO told him.

'Anything to say?' the executive officer asked.

'I slept in, sir.'

The executive officer was a lieutenant commander. He lifted his eyes to stare at me with chilly disdain. I was just another sailor as far as he was concerned. He wasn't interested in where I'd been, what had happened to me, just that I'd broken the rules.

'One day's pay, one day's leave,' he said.

'Aye aye, sir.'

I saluted, about-faced and marched away. I couldn't believe it. I'd lost one day's pay and one day's leave, both of which were in short enough supply as it was. To add insult to injury, later that day I was told I wouldn't be going on leave. Instead, I was posted to barracks. My official barracks was HMS *Drake* in Devonport near Plymouth, because that's where I'd done my training in 1939. So, with no opportunity to go home again, I left *Dragon* and went straight to Lime Street Station to catch a train south. I was pretty low when I got to *Drake*. The weather was gloomy and no one seemed to know why I was there. A doctor examined me in a desultory fashion, prodding and poking me a bit. Then he struck a match and held it in front of my face.

'What do you see?' he asked.

'A match, sir,' I replied.

'What sort of match?'

'A burning match, sir.' I had no idea what he was getting at.

'Are you sure?'

'Very sure, sir. It's a burning match.'

'Very good. That's all,' the doctor said. I came to the conclusion that he didn't know what he was getting at either.

After that mystifying episode I did general duties around the barracks, trying to give the impression that I had a real reason to be there. When they finally gave me Christmas leave, less one day and one day's pay of course, I caught the train back to Liverpool.

That Christmas of 1942 was wonderful and difficult at the same time. I found a brief peace, surrounded by loving faces and laughter. Despite Britain's austere wartime food rationing, my mother managed to conjure up the most delicious meals. I mostly spent my days sleeping and chatting with my family. I told them the barest details about the sinking, the German U-boat, the lifeboat voyage to Africa, and how one of the survivors had been a nurse named Doris Hawkins. They didn't press me for more. I suppose they thought I would tell them everything in my own time.

But quite often I sank deep into myself, swamped by a debilitating vagueness. I sat slumped in a chair for hours on end, not quite knowing who or where I was. My family had enough sense to leave me to myself as I drifted into unwanted daydreams about that wretched lifeboat, adrift once more on the Atlantic swell. I could actually smell the salt and feel the blistering tropical sun. Then some noisy activity or conversation elsewhere in the house would intrude and I'd claw myself back to the present, drained and depressed.

One afternoon there was a knock at the door and I opened it to find an American sailor standing there. I looked at him blankly. He looked back at me with his mouth wide open.

'Jesus, Mac. I thought you were dead!'

'Hello,' I said, puzzled about how an American sailor could possibly know my name. He broke into a laugh, which my fuddled brain vaguely recognised.

'Johnny?' I queried, looking more closely at him.

'You've lost weight,' Johnny Hennessey said.

'Bloody hell, I can't believe it's you. I thought you were dead, too.'

'Fancy a pint?' he asked.

'I fancy a dozen! What are you doing in the Yank navy?'

We caught a bus into the city and, when we'd got ourselves nicely settled into a pub, Johnny confessed that he'd really come to the house to see my mother and father.

'I came to tell them I thought you were definitely dead.'

'Cheery bastard,' I laughed. However, his thoughtfulness and the effort he'd obviously made to find out where my mother and father lived touched me.

'I thought they'd like to know you were up on the stern with me when the poor old *Laconia* started to go down.'

'That was a moment and a half, wasn't it?'

'Bloody shocking.'

'You still haven't answered my question,' I said.

'What question is that, then?'

'How you came by that Yank uniform.'

Like me, Johnny really didn't want to talk about what had happened. All he told me was that the Vichy French cruiser *Gloire* had eventually picked him up. It already had a large number of survivors on board. It took them to North Africa, first to Dakar and then on to Casablanca where they were interned in a prison camp. In November, some two months after the sinking, the camp had been liberated by the Americans. By then Johnny couldn't walk because one of his legs was badly infected from a scorpion bite, so the Americans took him to a US navy ship that was preparing to sail for Norfolk, Virginia.

'Went all the way to America in the sick bay. First class, it was. They gave me this uniform and I thought, well, they've got plenty of others just like it so I never gave it back!'

'Quite right, too.'

We drank a lot of beer, which fooled us into believing that the whole thing hadn't been quite so bad after all, and staggered out of the pub, arms around each other, talking nonsense and slurring futile promises to stay in touch. It was the last we ever saw of each other.

My much-needed leave ended in January 1943, when I was sent south to a shore establishment at St Austell in Cornwall, HMS *Vulcan*. Before long I was posted north, to a place called Afonwen near Pwllheli in North Wales, which was a Royal Navy recruit-training establishment. It also seemed to serve as a collecting house for survivors, and people who could only be described as bomb happy, those who had been broken by the strain of combat. I certainly qualified for the first category, possibly even the second. Over the entrance gates to the camp was a sign proclaiming it to be HMS *Glendower*.

The camp, which before the war had been one of Butlin's holiday camps, overlooked the lovely beach that swept around Cardigan Bay for over five miles. The scenery was spectacular, with Mount Snowden clearly visible in the distance. Recruits in their brand new uniforms were everywhere, doing drill and dashing about looking all shiny and enthusiastic. There was a contingent of women in the camp, too, members of the Women's Royal Navy Service, who were always simply known as Wrens.

Several doctors gave me another cursory examination when I arrived, but they didn't ask me about my time in the lifeboat, or offer any help or advice. I was put under the command of a leading seaman who went by the rather charming name of John Rainbow.

'Mac, you'll be the sentry for the Wrens' quarters.'

'All right.'

It could've been worse, I suppose. Rainbow didn't give me any instructions so, armed with a rifle, I spent my time patrolling the barbed wire fence that surrounded the Wrens' quarters. The Wrens came in and out, going about their business, and they were pretty easy on the eye. I didn't have the faintest idea what I was protecting them from and I'm quite sure my skin-and-bone presence and vague expression did nothing to reassure them.

Sentry duty didn't exactly stimulate my mind, so I kept drifting off to places I really didn't want to go. The camp and Wrens frequently disappeared from my mind and I would find myself below in *Laconia* as the torpedoes struck her, or being hauled aboard Hartenstein's U-boat, or frantically swimming to the lifeboat.

But I was in good company at *Glendower*, because many of the experienced sailors in the camp were in a pretty bad way, traumatised for one reason or another. We never talked about what had happened to us, and just tried to make the best of it. Sometimes a group of us would get passes to leave camp and we'd set off on foot, keen to have a look around, although our main ambition was usually to find a pub.

The countryside was very peaceful, the winter air smelling of farm animals and the tang of an occasional sea fret drifting in from Cardigan Bay. But other than those pleasant excursions, there seemed no purpose to anything. Being ashore didn't bother me at all because I felt certain I wouldn't survive another stint at sea, but not knowing what the navy had planned for me was hard. I was a shore-bound sailor with no ship, no real job and no hope. That is, until early in 1944 when they sent me south again to *Drake*. More doctors examined me. They said little and explained even less. I was assigned to general duties, and I wondered if I'd somehow slipped through the cracks of officialdom, that my records had been lost and no one even knew where I was anymore. It was a bleak period of my life. I had gone from being adrift on the Atlantic to being adrift on land.

Sometime during March, I was posted to another general duties job at the naval dockyards in Devonport, not far from *Drake*. I would report for duty late in the afternoon and work through the night, running messages, saluting the officers and generally doing what was asked of me. It wasn't hard. I was billeted in a schoolhouse on a hill beyond the dockyard, quietly settling into a routine without anyone bothering me too much. Occasionally I'd go home to Liverpool on a weekend pass.

During one of those weekends at home, I was sitting in a chair with my mind wandering as usual, when my father gave me an envelope. It was addressed to me in handwriting I didn't recognise.

'This came for you,' he said and then quietly left the room. There was a carefully penned letter inside:

Dear 'McLoughlin',

I automatically write the familiar name by which I knew you in those days and nights during which we tossed on the Atlantic, but somehow I feel that back in civilisation 'James' would be more suitable.

It was so kind of your father to write, & I was very very glad to hear of you again. I am sending you a copy of the booklet which I was persuaded to write. I think that I am glad now that I have done it as it seems to have helped many people. Do let me know what you think of it, & whether it gives a true picture of our experiences for you too.

If you have the addresses of any of the other survivors do please let me know & I will send each a copy.

I am glad to hear that you are well & working again. So am I, but I never forget, & I am sure you cannot either.

I hope that one day we shall meet again – you were always so kind & helpful to me & always looked after me whenever possible, & I am so grateful for those memories in the midst of many that I would rather not have.

With the very best of good wishes.

Yours very sincerely,

Doris M. Hawkins,
'Freckles'

I had tears in my eyes as I read those words. The whole dreadful experience overwhelmed me once more. I sat alone with the letter in my lap for quite a long time, and then read it again. It finally sank in that my father had written to Doris off his own bat, based on the scant information I had given him, to let her know that I was all right.

When he came back into the room he showed me another letter from Freckles, which she had addressed to him. In it she spoke of me in a way that I think made him very proud. She told him that she was doing full-time nursing work again as Sister in the Maternity Department of her own hospital, St Thomas's, which had been evacuated from London to Woking for the duration of the war. She wrote, too, of how much it had pained her that she'd been unable to do much for us in the lifeboat.

'She sent us two copies of her little book,' my father said. 'One for your mother and I, one for you.'

'I don't feel up to reading it just now,' I admitted.

'*Atlantic Torpedo* is what she's called it. Read it when you're ready, lad. When you're good and ready.'

'Sometime later.'

'No rush.'

'No.'

'She seems a decent person.'

I couldn't find the words to tell him just how incredibly decent Doris was. We both wrote a short letter back to her, and I felt guilty that I couldn't comment on her account of our voyage. I hoped she would read between the lines and understand why I didn't mention it, that I didn't have the mental strength to read it.

Even though her letter dredged the experience back to the surface, I found comfort in the fact that I wasn't alone in struggling with the awful memories. That was something positive to take back to my work in Devonport, where the dockyard was really bustling. We didn't know it at the time, but the build up to the D-day invasion of Europe was in full swing, with shipping of all kinds in very high demand. This attracted attention from the Germans, who mounted a number of bombing raids, usually in the early evenings.

Late one afternoon in early June I reported for my shift, half expecting an air raid a little later. Even though air raid shelters were scattered around the dockyard, a group of us always gathered in a room on the ground floor of the signals building. It was dangerous and against regulations, but we would sit there for ages with nothing to do while the bombs went off. On this particular afternoon I figured it would help pass the time if I could get hold of a good magazine to read. So I went upstairs where I'd seen a collection on previous visits. A Wren was operating the switchboard there. She was absolutely gorgeous.

'Can I borrow one of the magazines?' I asked her.

'No,' she said in a very haughty fashion.

'I just want to have something to read if the Germans come over.'

'No,' she said again.

'I'll return it, you know, after the all clear.' I really wanted that magazine.

'All right,' the Wren finally said. I thought she only relented because she was busy and wanted to get rid of me.

Sure enough there was an air raid, a pretty big one that went on for a long time and caused quite a lot of damage. I sat it out reading my magazine and thinking about the Wren on the switchboard. After it was over I went back to my work until early the next morning. I was just getting ready to go off duty when I remembered the magazine, so I went back up the stairs of the signals building, where the Wren appeared to be finishing her shift as well.

'Just returning the magazine,' I told her.

'Good,' she said.

'You finishing up now?'

'Yes.'

'Can I walk you back to your billet?'

'Oh, yes, I suppose so,' the Wren said. Her earlier haughtiness had dissolved somewhat because she was going off duty.

We picked our way through the bomb damage and dodged the fire engines entering the dockyard, chatting quietly. I was instantly at ease with her. She was no longer the business-like Wren on duty at her switchboard, more like a normal friendly girl. She told me her name was Dorothy Field and that she was 19. When we got to her billet I knew I had to do something right there and then.

'Would you like to go out with me?' I asked.

'I've got a boyfriend.'

'Oh.'

'A Royal Marine. He's away at sea, on HMS *Black Prince*,' she said. I knew *Black Prince* was a cruiser.

'I see.'

'I would like to go out with you, though. Just as a friend, mind,' she said. 'That would be nice.'

'All right,' I said. I felt wonderful.

Some very special chemistry was at work between us, I knew that for certain, despite the fact that she had a boyfriend. We began our friendship by going for long walks on Plymouth Hoe and various other places in and around Plymouth itself. Then we started to meet for cups of tea at a cafe called The Magnet, which was apt because

I was very strongly drawn to this beautiful young woman. Friendship was unexpectedly becoming something more.

Plymouth was pretty much a military city at that stage of the war, swarming with people in uniform, so privacy was hard to come by, especially for two young people living in separate billets. Our lodgings were always noisy, with people coming and going at odd hours of the day and night, so I suggested to Dorothy that we meet in the nearby cemetery. It was the only quiet place I could think of.

'Very romantic,' she said.

We'd meet in the cemetery and, strange to think of it now, we fell in love among the headstones. I couldn't believe my good fortune. As for telling her about my experiences in the navy, I merely mentioned that my ship had been torpedoed and that I'd been in a lifeboat for a while, then left it at that. I must have hid my trauma well.

'You're such a happy-go-lucky sailor!' she told me.

After several weeks of walks, cups of tea and meeting in the cemetery, Dorothy invited me to her family home in Totnes to meet her parents. A chap knew things were pretty serious in those days if a girl asked him home to meet her parents. They were lovely people, but I don't think they were overly impressed that their daughter was involved with a sailor, let alone one who was obviously a little vague and confused.

A few weeks after meeting Dorothy's parents I received a draft chit, ordering me to join the aircraft carrier HMS *Implacable*. They sent me on leave for about 10 days before I was due to join the ship at Scapa Flow in Scotland. I was anxious about this, because I didn't know how long

I would be away, so I took Dorothy for another walk on Plymouth Hoe. There were a number of Royal Navy vessels riding at anchor in Plymouth Sound, from where I'd first gone to sea on HMS *Valiant* nearly five years before. It was about as traditional a British naval scene as I could imagine. Sir Francis Drake, Sir Walter Raleigh and all the other Elizabethan naval heroes had stood on this very spot before setting sail on their great voyages.

'Will you marry me?' I asked. I had little time to waste, so there was no point in beating about the bush.

'Yes,' Dorothy said straight away.

'That's good.'

'But my parents will never agree. After all, we've only known each other for a few weeks,' she gently reminded me.

'What are we going to do then?'

'I can get some leave as well. I'll come with you to Liverpool and we'll just go ahead and get married,' she said calmly.

Without telling her parents, Dorothy joined me on my leave. We went to my parents' house in Liverpool, where I introduced her to the family. When I told them we were going to be married there were some worried comments about not knowing each other long enough and that it wouldn't last. Naturally we ignored all of it because we knew we loved each other and simply wanted to be together. After they'd recovered from the shock, my family threw themselves into the moment with good humour and enthusiasm. We made arrangements for a simple wedding service in All Saints, Speke, the church right next door to my parents' house. Dorothy and I exchanged our vows on 12 September, 1944. We'd known each other for just 12 weeks. It was the happiest day of my life and, by a strange coincidence, it was exactly two years after the very worst day of my life, the day *Laconia* was torpedoed in the Atlantic.

After the ceremony we went back to the house, where we had our honeymoon. I showed Dorothy the sights of Liverpool, such as they were. Then my leave was over and I left to join *Implacable*. It was a painful parting. Dorothy caught a train south to break the news of our marriage to her family in Totnes, while I caught one north to Scotland. We didn't know when we'd see each other again. Our situation was nothing unusual, though. A live-today-for-tomorrow-we-die attitude was strong among young people at that time. Many couples were getting married quickly, then being parted even quicker as their lives were tossed upside down by the instant demands of wartime postings. Everyone was affected in some way and teary railway station farewells were commonplace. Liverpool's Lime Street Station was, it seemed to me, the saddest of places.

If I had been overawed by *Valiant* when I first joined her in 1939, then I was completely overwhelmed by *Implacable*. She was a brand new carrier, fresh out of the shipyards and just commissioned. Her flight deck was nearly 800 feet long and 100 wide. She displaced about 33,000 tons fully loaded and could steam at 32 knots. On 20 September 1944, I was just one sailor in a new crew of 1500 officers and men who came aboard to take her on her first operational cruise. Also on board was a 700-strong Fleet Air Arm contingent charged with maintaining and flying her aircraft, a mixture of Seafires and Barracudas. I had only been on board a few hours when someone told me *Implacable* had a range of 11,000 nautical miles. I winced. We could be going just about anywhere in the world. But as it turned out we were only heading to Norway on an anti-shipping operation.

I didn't know a soul on board. I was assigned to the wireless operators' mess and only a short while after we put to sea I could feel myself slipping into a most dreadful state. I was beside myself with anxiety about the possibility of a torpedo attack. If ever there was a juicy target for a German U-boat, it was an aircraft carrier. The thought of *Implacable* sinking almost immobilised me, and I realised that I had to do something about the way I was feeling.

With a great deal of trepidation, I went to see the surgeon-commander, the senior medical officer. But I was lucky. He was a kind, gentle officer who asked me a lot of questions about the sinking of *Laconia*, my time in the lifeboat and what I was feeling. He listened patiently for quite a long time as I did my best to explain it all.

'These experiences take time to get over. You're stuck on board for the moment, so stay with it as best you can,' he said.

'Aye aye, sir.'

'Come and see me in my quarters at any time.'

At least there was someone who understood a little of my fears. So I went about my duties, trying to suppress a boiling anxiety, my health slowly deteriorating.

After four weeks of aircraft operations off Norway, during which we hit very heavy sea conditions, *Implacable* returned to Scotland to have some weather damage repaired.

The surgeon-commander must have had significant influence because as soon as the carrier docked, the master-at-arms gave me a chit posting me back to barracks. So I returned to *Drake* and had a wonderful reunion with Dorothy. She had plenty to tell me. She had received her discharge papers from the Wrens.

'Oh, and I'm pregnant,' she announced.

I was amazed at her calmness about such a momentous occasion. To begin with I was overwhelmed, but then an extraordinary happiness and contentment rushed through me. I couldn't keep the smile off my face. Becoming a father was just what I needed. It gave me something special to think about, something positive for the future instead of dwelling on the past.

However, it seemed the navy still had no real plans for me, except perhaps to give me some easy duty after my miserable spell on *Implacable*. Another doctor examined me half-heartedly, and I got the impression that he thought I was bomb happy. Then I was relieved to be posted to the Royal Naval College, which had been moved to Chester from its traditional home in Dartmouth, to reduce the risk of bombing. So I went north once again, leaving Dorothy in the care of her parents. It was nearly Christmas, 1944.

The College had taken over a stately country mansion with magnificent manicured gardens. Everything about the place was immaculate, traditional and very spit-and-polish. My job was that of sailor-servant to an elderly officer who had served at sea in World War One, returned to civilian life between the wars, then rejoined the Royal Navy at the start of hostilities in 1939. He had private quarters tucked away in the old mansion and gave me instructions while warming his feet in front of a homely open fire. I ran his messages, made sure people reported to him when they were required, and generally looked after him. I could never quite work out what his job was, which was fitting really because I wasn't sure what mine was either.

In posting me to Chester the navy had done me something of a favour, because it wasn't far to Liverpool by train and I could easily get home to see my family whenever I got a 12-hour pass. After a while it became a rather pleasant routine, marred only by the fact that I desperately wanted to return to Dorothy. Another small difficulty was that the College was nine miles from the Chester railway station. When my leave was over, I would have to run back to the College for fear of being late and getting docked leave and pay again. It improved my fitness and general health no end, that did.

I had just begun to enjoy the posting in Chester when the navy sent me back to *Drake* where I was drafted to an establishment I'd never heard of, HMS *Golden Hind*.

'Where's *Golden Hind*?' I asked.

'Sydney.'

'Where?'

'Sydney in Australia.'

'Australia! I can't go to bloody Australia, I've got a pregnant wife!'

'You'll go where the chit says.'

13

A sea change far away

It was hard to grasp that I was being sent about as far away from England as it was possible to go.

'They must know what they're doing,' Dorothy told me when I broke the news to her.

'I doubt it,' I said.

Although unhappy about this posting, Dorothy took the news in her stride, resigned like so many other service wives to the routine disturbances of life. Her confidence that everything would work out all right helped ease my concerns.

I joined a ship called *Dominion Monarch* in Southhampton in February 1945. She was a luxury Shaw Saville liner before the war, cruising regularly to Australia and New Zealand, but had been requisitioned by the Royal Navy to serve as a troopship. Stripped of all her pre-war luxury and painted a gloomy grey, she could carry over 3000 troops. Her sea-stained, war-weary appearance reminded me of how *Laconia* had looked when I went aboard her in Cape Town in 1942. The old anxieties gripped me again, but were quietened somewhat by the fact that I was taking passage for the first time. That was a change. So, I settled down to experience shipboard life without duties.

It was a reasonably pleasant six-week voyage. There

were personnel from all three British services on board, as well as many Australians, so there was no shortage of company and conversation. I shared a mess deck with a group of soldiers.

We were supposed to wash our own dishes after meals, and after only a week or so I noticed that the mess was running short of crockery. That puzzled me until I saw a soldier finish his meal, get up from the mess table and throw his dirty dishes through an open porthole.

We sailed south-west across the Atlantic and entered the Panama Canal near Colon. The trip along the canal intrigued me no end. It took an entire day to travel the 40 miles through the system of massive water-filled chambers and man-made lakes that raise and lower ships through the mountainous terrain of central Panama. We came out into the Pacific at Panama City and headed for Australia.

My intense fear of being below decks had not diminished, so I spent most of my time on the upper deck, idling away the hours reading and watching the sea. My mind wandered quite a lot. On several occasions I imagined I was on *Laconia* again, which sent a disturbing icy sensation through me. As we crossed the Pacific and the weather got warmer, I slept out on the deck most nights. I planned on being first over the side if something went wrong.

The *Dominion Monarch* sailed through Sydney Heads early on a lovely March day, and the sight of Sydney Harbour was absolutely beautiful. I recalled my father talking about its great coat-hanger bridge being built. Finally seeing it for myself created the strange notion that this was a homecoming of sorts.

We docked at Woollomooloo, where the wharf was swarming with people who'd come to see the ship berth. Among them were Sydney families selected to welcome servicemen to Australia, who came on board to introduce themselves. A middle-aged couple singled me out and greeted me like their long lost son, though they didn't know me from a bar of soap. He was a beefy bloke, a rough-and-ready signalman with the New South Wales Railways. She was a short, chunky woman. They both had, to my ears at least, the most extraordinary Australian accents.

'G'day mate, what's ya name?' the bloke asked.

'Jim. Everyone calls me Mac.'

''Ow yer goin' Mac, all right?' He shook my hand and almost crushed it.

'Fine thanks.'

'Meet me missus.'

''Ow yer goin' Mac, all right?' his wife asked.

'Fine thanks.'

'Want any washin' done?'

'Pardon?'

'Dirty clothes, love. I'll wash and iron 'em for ya.'

'It's no bloody trouble for the missus, Mac,' the bloke said.

'No, honestly,' I said. I couldn't believe the generosity of these people.

'Come on, then,' the woman said. 'Let's go 'ome and 'ave a cuppa an' a decent feed.'

I couldn't have wished for a warmer welcome. Those perfect strangers took me to their home where they produced the promised cup of tea and a meal, then entertained me with their easy going conversation for the rest of the day. They couldn't do enough for me. It was my first taste of genuine, no-questions-asked Australian mateship. Compared to the often-stifling English reserve I was accustomed to, their extroverted, carefree nature was a real eye opener. When it was dark they took me back to the *Dominion Monarch*.

The next morning I joined a big group of sailors on the wharf. A convoy of covered army trucks arrived and we all climbed aboard. I didn't have a clue where we were going, but it turned out to be to the Warwick Farm racecourse, which had been transformed into a massive tent city, a sort of mustering centre for navy personnel. I found myself in a tent with a few other blokes who were also wondering what the hell was going on. As usual, no one was telling us anything. A lot of complaining started up.

'So this is bloody Australia.'

'End of the earth, this is.'

'Wonder when the next race starts.'

'Is this *Golden Hind*?' I asked.

'I think so.'

I spent a few miserable days at Warwick Farm with nothing to do, during which I sank into one of my dark, low moods, wondering why the navy had sent me all the way out here while I had a pregnant wife to take care of in England. The only worthwhile things in my life, my family and my wife and unborn child, were all on the other side of the world and it didn't make any sense at all. I was eventually ordered to report to the Royal Navy Hospital at Punchbowl, and the thought crossed my mind that I was going to be admitted as a patient. *Maybe this is the place where they treat survivors. Make a bit of sense, that would.* It was a rather appealing thought. I felt I could do with a spell in hospital.

I soon discovered that the Royal Navy Hospital, like Warwick Farm, came under the banner of HMS *Golden Hind.* And no, I wasn't there as a patient. The navy had more important things in mind for me.

'You'll be on the sentry detail, Mac.'

'All right.'

So there I was, manning the front gate of the Royal Navy Hospital in Australia. It was like a bad practical joke. There were other survivors there, blokes who had emerged from similar disasters at sea, only to find themselves adrift with no real job. No one on the medical staff interviewed me or showed the slightest interest in why I was there. So I just got on with it, all the time thinking about Dorothy and hoping everything was fine back in England. I was very worried about her because we'd been hearing reports of deadly German V2 rockets creating havoc and terror over London and parts of southern England. I did my sentry duty and the time passed slowly. There were only Dorothy's letters to look forward to.

The easy-going Australian way of life seeped into me. The weather in Sydney was sunny and warm, even as winter approached. On my days off I'd team up with a few other sailors and go into the city. Naturally we'd do the rounds of the pubs and then, more often than not, we'd wander down to Circular Quay. I thought of my father quite a bit as I watched the ferries come and go. He had always told me what a great place Australia was, and I could only agree. People were friendly and open. Despite the war, they had a cheeriness and optimism that I found very appealing. I was fascinated by the expression 'She'll be right, mate!' I heard it often.

One night I was with a couple of other sailors in the city. We'd had a bit to drink. Well, a hell of a lot, actually. When it was time to make our way back to *Golden Hind* we stumbled onto a crowded train going to Punchbowl. The rhythm of the train was very soothing and within a few minutes we were all asleep, chins on our chests and dribbling out the sides of our mouths in the true tradition of drunken sailors. After what seemed like just a few minutes we woke up. The train had stopped and it was pitch black. Everything was strangely silent.

'Where the friggin' hell are we?'

Someone lit a match. In its weak light we could see that our carriage was completely empty.

'There's another train right alongside us,' I offered.

'Don't tell me . . .'

'We're in the bloody train depot!'

'We're in deep trouble, that's what we're in.'

'What time is it?'

Another match spluttered. We leant into its light and looked at our watches. It was after two o'clock in the morning.

'Why the hell didn't someone wake us up?'

'Bloody useless Australians.'

'We'll be up on report for this.'

We groped our way along the carriage until we found a door and then lowered ourselves onto the tracks.

'Got any idea how to get to the hospital from here?'

'How the hell would I know? I'm a stranger in a strange land.'

'Only asking.'

We stumbled around the depot for a bit, tripping over railway lines and cursing until we eventually saw a light in a building. There was a night watchman on duty inside. When we explained our predicament he just laughed and gave us directions back to *Golden Hind*. It was a pretty long walk. We were exhausted when we arrived at the front gate, and completely sober, too. Fortunately, one of our mates was on sentry duty and he let us in, no questions asked. We didn't hear anything about it the next day, as the barracks were swept up in celebration.

It was 8 May, V-E Day. Germany had surrendered and the war in Europe was over. The relief was enormous. Dorothy was safe and surely, surely, the navy would send us all home. But they didn't, of course, because the war against Japan was still dragging on.

So I guarded the gate in front of the Royal Navy Hospital until, early in August, a telegram came from Dorothy, telling me that I was the father of a baby boy called Barry. I was overjoyed at the news, but filled with heartache at being so far away. It made me even more desperate to get home. Then on 15 August, we heard the astonishing news that the Americans had dropped atomic bombs on Hiroshima and Nagasaki, and that the Japanese had surrendered. I was in Martin Place as the city erupted into the wildest celebration imaginable. V-J Day in Sydney was one big wonderful party, chaotic with uniforms and streamers and people hugging and kissing complete strangers.

Later in the day I went to the harbour. There were a lot of warships there, including the aircraft carrier HMS *Indomitable*, sister to *Implacable*, my last ship. It was strange to think that after nearly six years of vital work those great fighting ships and all the sailors serving on them no longer had such urgent purpose. I had no desire whatsoever to go to sea again, but I had to get home somehow.

August drifted into September and the buzz round the hospital was different every day. We heard that hostilities-only personnel would be demobbed from the navy in Australia. Then the word was that they would be posted back to England and demobbed there. Then there were whispers that we would all be posted to Japan. More than a few English sailors had fallen for Australian girls and wanted to stay. Some had even taken the unlawful step of going absent without leave to stay with their new loves. I had to complete my seven years' service though, because I'd joined before the war started. But how and where I had no idea. The only certainty, it seemed to me, was that the war was over.

It wasn't until early October that I got a draft chit. My heart was in my mouth when I read it. HMS *Indomitable*, the aircraft carrier I'd seen in Sydney Harbour.

Here we go again!

There was nothing on the draft chit to indicate where *Indomitable* would be sailing. Maybe the rumour about going to Japan was true. Anyway, I went aboard and handed my draft chit to the master-at-arms.

'McLoughlin, is it?'

'Yes, sir.'

'Let's see what we've got in store for you.'

I could hardly breath or swallow as he flicked through his paperwork.

'Demob,' he said.

'Yes, sir. Ship going to England, sir?'

'Where else would it be going, the bleedin' South Pole?'

I went to my mess in shock. I was being demobbed without having to serve out my seven years. The relief was overwhelming. I couldn't wait to get out of the navy and back to my home. I knew it had to be a mistake, but if someone had buggered up the paperwork I wasn't about to tell them. As the carrier steamed out through Sydney Heads I wondered if I'd ever see Australia again. Although I desperately wanted to get home to Dorothy and my newborn son, I knew that I would miss the place.

Once again the navy didn't seem to know what to do with me. I didn't have any duties on board, so I couldn't keep my mind calm. I imagined submarines lurking about, commanded by fanatical Japanese commanders who either didn't know the war was over or just refused to accept it. I spent my time avoiding the lower decks or seeking out vantage points to watch the flying operations.

Indomitable had already been at sea for several weeks when I was summoned to appear before the commander-writer, the ship's senior clerk. He was angry.

'What the hell are you doing, McLoughlin?'

'Nothing, sir.' This was quite accurate.

'I mean, what the hell are you doing on this ship?' I thought that was a bloody stupid question. I was on this ship because the Royal Navy had posted me to it.

'My draft chit said to report to *Indomitable*, sir.'

'Do you realise you're not due for demob?'

'No,' I lied.

'You signed on for seven years.'

'Yes, sir.'

'Only people being demobbed should be coming back with us. You were supposed to stay in Australia.'

'But I'm here, sir.'

'I can see that. Well, I'm sure the captain won't be turning about on your behalf so you'll just have to carry on.'

'Aye aye, sir.'

Nothing more was said so I carried on doing what I'd been doing before, which was nothing, and in that strange state of limbo I arrived home in time to spend Christmas leave 1945 with Dorothy and Barry. I was in awe of the little human miracle we had created together. It was the most marvellous feeling to hold him. The responsibility I felt for my very own family would, I hoped, sustain me and help push unwelcome memories deep, deep into the background.

My service finally ended at Plymouth in 1946. I gave my uniform back to the Royal Navy and they swapped it for a pinstripe suit and a suitcase. Everyone was given that.

'We won't put you on the Fleet Reserve,' they told me. They didn't say why, but I had a fair idea. They thought I was bomb happy.

'That suits me,' I said, and gladly left the service I'd been so desperate to join seven years before.

The only thing I had to put in my free suitcase was my free pinstripe suit, but I didn't have anything else to wear, so I walked away from the navy depot a free man in a badly cut suit clutching an empty suitcase. I didn't have a clue how I would support my family or what to do with the rest of my life. I just hoped something would turn up.

14
Postscript to a nightmare

We settled down to post-war life in the Devon town of Totnes where Dorothy's parents lived. My father-in-law had a shoe-making business in the main street and we set up house in a second-floor flat above a hairdresser's salon, directly across the street from his shop.

My main concern was finding a job. I had a wife and child to support, but all I knew were ships and ships' guns, so I was really starting from scratch. There was a lot of talk about there being a building boom because the war was over, so I decided to become a bricklayer. I found work as a builder's labourer, earning a pittance, while I was doing a bricklaying course in Plymouth. It was getting near Christmas 1946 and it was freezing. Believe me, there is no more miserable place than a building site in the middle of a bitter British winter. I dug trenches, filled wheelbarrows with dirt, carried bricks, mixed concrete, dug more trenches and daydreamed about summer in Australia. With hands bleeding from handling the bricks, I knew straight off that I wasn't cut out for that line of work, but there didn't seem to be many other opportunities.

I was getting pretty worried because Dorothy was now expecting our second child. One day I was walking down the main street of Totnes, wondering where I was going to find a better job, when I noticed the local policeman, a terrific chap called Ken Alway, walking toward me. He was pulling a hand trolley with a large canvas bag on it. When he saw me he stopped for a chat, which he liked to do. As the town's copper, Ken knew and talked to everyone and was well respected.

'What have you got there, Ken?'

'Oh, it's just a body.'

'What!'

'Taking it down to the morgue.'

'You mean a *dead* body?'

'Well, I wouldn't be taking a live one down to the morgue, now would I?'

'No, suppose you wouldn't be.'

Ken and I stood there in the main street for a while chatting about this and that, accompanied by the recently departed soul on the trolley. People were walking past, going about their business, oblivious to Ken's macabre cargo.

'Afternoon, Ken!' a passer-by called out.

'Hello there,' Ken replied. 'Family well?'

'Very well, thanks.'

'Listen, Mac,' Ken said, turning back to me. 'I've noticed you're looking a bit miserable these days. Everything all right?'

'No, as a matter of fact,' I told him. 'I've got this job as a builder's labourer. Bloody terrible it is.'

'You know, I think you'd make a good country copper.'

'Me? A copper? Don't be daft.'

'You should think about it. It's a good life. Good people around you, interesting work.'

I glanced at his trolley, wondering if I could be that casual if I had to trundle a dead body along the main street.

'All right, Ken. I'll think about it.'

I went home and told Dorothy about Ken and his dead body. We had a good laugh. When I mentioned his suggestion of becoming a policeman, she said it would suit me more than being a bricklayer. The more trenches I dug the more I agreed. So, a few days later I went to the Totnes police station and filled out an application form. I wasn't really expecting anything to come of it, so I was surprised and relieved to get an interview with the Assistant Chief Constable at police headquarters in Exeter. It went well and I was accepted into the Devon Constabulary. I was over the moon. *For once I might do some work that has real human value.* The injustices I'd seen while in the lifeboat still angered me, especially the fact that people had perished horribly for want of stolen emergency rations.

I began my police training in March 1947, at the Falfield Police Training School near Bristol. Most of my fellow recruits were ex-servicemen who, like me, found something oddly reassuring about being back in uniform. While I was away on the three-month training course, Dorothy gave birth to our second son, Ian. It was a demanding time, but I felt a great sense of pride in what I was doing. I got a good result at the end of the course, graduating as a probationary constable.

Life as a country copper was many things, but it was never dull! I was mostly assigned to bicycle patrols, pedalling far and wide around the Devon countryside, policing the rural communities surrounding Totnes, Kingsbridge and the picture-postcard villages of Aveton Gifford, Lodiswell and Harbertonford. It was routine most of the time, dealing with petty theft, road accidents, traffic control and infringements of the various livestock acts, although I once arrested an escapee from Dartmoor prison and on another occasion, with trembling knees, managed to pacify a man who had gone berserk wielding a large carving knife. It was a bit like living in an episode of that wonderful television series *Heartbeat*, because in every town and village there seemed to be a Greengrass-like character intent on testing the will and wits of the local police.

During that period Dorothy presented me with two more beautiful children, with Judith arriving in 1951 and Jane in 1953. The war slipped into the background, although terrible memories still surfaced in my sleep from time to time. I was particularly disturbed by a recurring nightmare about being below decks in *Laconia* as the torpedoes struck her. In the pitch black and screaming chaos I struggled to climb the Jacob's ladder to safety. Then I would snap awake in a blind panic, sweating profusely, legs kicking wildly. It always left me wide-eyed and exhausted. That nightmare has continued to disturb my sleep, and Dorothy's, ever since.

Sometimes I'd be going about my duties when incredibly vivid memories of the lifeboat would come out of nowhere. I'd see gallant Doctor Purslow saying goodbye to us and then falling backwards over the gunwale. I'd hear poor Mickey pleading for his life. I'd see Hartenstein saluting from his conning tower, and the freckles on Doris's round face. They made me terribly sad, those memories, but at the same time immensely thankful to be alive and cycling through the lovely hills of Devon.

I think it was about five years after the war ended that I finally steeled myself to read Doris's account of those terrible events. Her tiny book *Atlantic Torpedo* was a very eloquent, gentle and understated description of what had occurred in the lifeboat. Her writing confirmed that she was an extraordinarily kind and compassionate person. It reminded me of many incidents that I had been trying to forget, but also many that I found pleasure in remembering.

While we were living in Totnes, Dorothy and I would sometimes go to Liverpool to visit my family. On one of those trips I remembered that my old shipmate Peter Rimmer came from Southport, which is just outside Liverpool near the mouth of the River Mersey. It was Peter who had absolutely astonished me by rushing below decks to retrieve his collection of photographs when *Laconia* was sinking. I couldn't imagine how he had survived.

Dorothy and I went to Southport to find his family or at least someone who knew of him. Well, we found Peter Rimmer himself, just as tall and skinny as ever and living happily with his young wife, a lovely Irish girl called Bridie. We had a wonderful get together although, strangely, we didn't say very much about the sinking. Instead, Peter and I talked and laughed about the unexpected turns our lives had taken since the war, about how odd it was that I ended up a policeman and he a children's toy-maker. Sometime later he and Bridie called in to see us in Totnes.

By the end of 1954 I was constantly being distracted by thoughts of Australia. It was some 10 years since I'd been there and, although it had been a difficult time in my life, I thought fondly of the openness of the people, the informal way of life and the warm, sunny weather. This all came to a head when I was doing a daytime foot patrol in Harbertonford. I said hello to a chap in the street, who I hadn't seen around the village before, and when we stopped for a chat I detected a well-remembered accent.

'You Australian?' I asked him.

'Yeah,' he said. 'Originally from Devon, but I'm an Australian now. Lived there for most of my life. I'm just back for a visit.'

'I was there in the war,' I said.

We talked for quite a while, and he told me about all the opportunities in Australia.

'I like the sound of that.'

I wondered what sort of future might be in store for my family in England, where post-war austerity still held a tight, grey grip on everyone. *Things could be better for the children in Australia.* I imagined them running carefree on an Australian beach somewhere.

My career seemed to be in a rut. I'd passed the exams for promotion to sergeant, and been told that I was a first-class country policeman, but I was still a constable. I had a gnawing feeling that I'd never be anything more than a country copper, a little fish swimming round and round in the same small pond.

Dorothy and I talked about going to Kenya, but the violence of the Mau Mau uprising there put us off. A police officer I knew had left to join the police force out in Malaya, but that didn't appeal to us. We thought of Canada and America. But all the time I couldn't let go of the idea of Australia.

'Look,' I finally said. 'Let's just do it. Let's apply for Australia and see what happens.'

So we sent away for all the brochures on Australia, which showed the types of houses and schools available and, of course, the scenery and the beaches. In all the photographs there was never a cloud in the sky, and with those images dancing around in our minds we applied to emigrate to Australia. A letter came giving us the choice of settling in Rockhampton or Sydney. There was a mad scramble for the atlas to see where Rockhampton was.

'It'll be too hot there,' Dorothy said.

'Let's make it Sydney, then. I've been there, I know what it's like.'

So in 1955 we came to Australia with the children. It was, without doubt, the best thing we could have done. Dorothy fell in love with the way of life immediately and never looked back. After a short time in Sydney we moved to South Australia. Our fifth child, Diane, was born in Adelaide in 1960. I joined the South Australian Police Force, serving in uniform for 25 years and finally finishing my career as a sergeant in the Prosecution Division.

Epilogue

Dorothy and I live in Adelaide, where our home is often filled with the laughter and chatter of 10 grandchildren and three great-grandchildren. Our lounge room looks out onto a peaceful garden. It's a marvellous place to sit and read and think. In my retirement I've spent many, many hours doing both.

While this has invited the terrible memories back in, little by little I've discovered much about the *Laconia* incident and gained a sense of my small part in the bigger picture. The repercussions of that dreadful sinking have rippled out far beyond my life.

My journey of discovery began quite by accident, in March 1994, when I noticed a letter to the editor in the Adelaide *Advertiser* written by Professor Peter H Liddle of the University of Leeds. At that time he was the keeper of an archive at the university, known as the Liddle Collection, dedicated to preserving the war experiences of British and British Commonwealth men and women. The professor was seeking personal accounts and documentation that could be added to what was already a substantial amount of material.

Thinking he might be interested in something relating to the *Laconia* tragedy, I sent Peter a copy of Doris Hawkins'

Atlantic Torpedo with a brief note explaining that I had been in the lifeboat with her. He wrote back promptly, explaining how he had been deeply moved and humbled by her account. Then he went on to make, and heavily underline, a request that took me completely by surprise:

> *... however, will you not please consider writing your own account unless it would be too painful. My University would be honoured to have such an account and I would appreciate the labour in time, thought and physical effort ...*

After a time I concluded that I couldn't possibly add anything to what Doris had penned so many years ago. So I shot a note back to Peter telling him so. His response was swift, gently chastising and very determined:

> *You must not be allowed to escape so lightly!! I do not want, still less expect, a superb literary effort but I do think that you should try, in your own way to retell some of your memories. It is a way of ensuring that you leave a record of what you yourself went through – of your personal participation in so harrowing a collective experience. Come on now please – just do your best.*

So I reluctantly set about writing my own account. I found it a struggle. Throughout my career as a police officer I had written countless reports of criminal incidents that were required to be factual, unemotional and brief, but this was something entirely different. It was torture reliving those dreadful events, but by the middle of 1995 I'd managed to put it down. It ran to 18 typed pages, which seemed totally inadequate, but I breathed a sigh of relief when it was done. Just after I finished it, Dorothy and I were booked to fly to Britain to see relatives, so I decided to deliver the pages personally to Peter in Leeds. He seemed enormously pleased to receive them and we had a wonderful meeting at the university, after which Dorothy and I stayed overnight with he and his wife.

My brief personal account therefore joined the Liddle Collection where, in some small way, it has become part of the history of World War Two. I was chuffed. Sometime later a couple I knew through my church, Nicholas and Eveleen Kerr, kindly interviewed me and expanded my initial account into a longer and more satisfying document.

At my age, modern technology like the internet can be bewildering and intimidating. However, such things are part of every day life for my children and grandchildren who, once they had read my personal account of the *Laconia* sinking, began to send me all manner of fascinating information readily available through this mysterious 'world wide web'. Things I've long wondered about have been clarified.

For many years I had thought about Werner Hartenstein, about his kindness and courage. I harboured a vague idea of one day meeting him again and thanking him personally. However, with great sadness and regret, I learnt from an internet site devoted to the history of U-boats that he hadn't survived the war. On 8 March 1943, just six months after the sinking of *Laconia*, U-156 was east of Barbados where it was detected by a US Catalina aircraft. Depth charges were dropped on the submarine, which was destroyed with the loss of all 52 of her crew. I wept for Hartenstein and his men because they were sailors just like me, who took me aboard their vessel when I was in dire straits and, in so doing, put themselves in harm's way. Hartenstein had turned 35 just a few days before his death.

Then I learnt that, just seven days after sinking *Laconia*, Hartenstein attacked and sank another vessel, an armed merchant ship called *Quebec City*. Once again he showed compassion for the survivors at great risk to himself, this time bringing his submarine alongside a crowded lifeboat, which contained the captain of *Quebec City*. Hartenstein invited the merchant ship's captain aboard U-156 so he could study nautical charts and plot an accurate course to the African coast. Telling the captain that the Americans had bombed him the previous week while helping *Laconia* survivors, he apologised for not being able to render further assistance. As he reluctantly set the lifeboat adrift, he called out to its occupants:

'A good journey and a safe landing. We hope to meet you again in a better and more peaceful world.'

David C Jones, one of 21 people in that lifeboat who survived to reach the coast of Africa, not very far from where my own group of survivors made landfall, described this incident in his book *The Enemy We Killed, My Friend*. It proved to me beyond doubt that Werner Hartenstein was an extraordinarily honourable man who, at a time of massive conflict and inhumanity, had the courage to do what was morally right even though it might have been militarily unwise.

Captain Erich Wurdermann, commander of U-506, also risked his boat in the chaotic effort to help *Laconia* survivors aboard. He responded to Hartenstein's radio message, and was the first to reach U-156.

I also discovered what became of HMS *Valiant*. The damage caused by the Italian frogmen in Alexandria Harbour was repaired and she continued to serve with distinction. In 1943 she supported the Allied invasions of Sicily and Salerno and, when Italy surrendered, escorted the Italian fleet into Malta. In August 1944, she was badly damaged in a dry-dock accident in Ceylon, which resulted in her returning to England for extensive repairs that were not completed until after the war. She finished her days as a training ship, finally being sold for scrap in 1948. I felt this was a less than noble end for such a fine ship. However, her name lives on. Today, HMS *Valiant* is one of the Royal Navy's nuclear submarines.

Valiant's young Air Defence Officer, Prince Philip of Greece, was mentioned in dispatches for his skilful coordination of the ship's searchlights during our action against the Italians in the Battle of Matapan. Later he was awarded the Greek War Cross of Valour and, of course, went on to marry Britain's Queen Elizabeth the Second, becoming Prince Philip, the Duke of Edinburgh.

The internet also informed me that the battleship that had so inspired me to join the Royal Navy, HMS *Royal Oak*, is still lying on the bottom of Scapa Flow where she was sunk in the first few weeks of the war. There has been much discussion in recent years about what to do with the wreck because oil is still seeping from her and causing serious environmental concerns. It is a sensitive issue because 800 sailors died inside her and she remains an official war grave.

A couple of years after meeting Peter Liddle in Leeds, Dorothy and I were in England once again. One day we went for a walk on Plymouth Hoe, to the very spot where I had proposed to her in 1944. We looked quietly at the cenotaph there that lists the names of Royal Navy personnel lost at sea in times of war. So many, many names. One of them was Mickey's, and I became very emotional because I could still hear him pleading not to be thrown overboard.

Also during this trip we spent time trying to trace Doris. We went first to the address in Woking, Surrey, from her letter to me in 1944, but she wasn't known there. We checked with the Medical Board and also Guy's Hospital in London but there was no record of her to be found. I knew that she would have long retired from her profession of nursing, so I wasn't entirely surprised. I came home resigned to the fact that I'd probably never know what happened to her.

However, in 2000 I came across a book called *The Sinking of The Laconia* by the late Reverend Frederick Grossmith, who had researched the sinking in immense detail. From this book I learnt that Doris Hawkins OBE had died in 1991 at the age of 80. I read this with a heavy heart. However, it appeared that her own book had achieved a great deal. In it, she had criticised the way lifeboats were equipped. She wrote that it ought to be compulsory for lifeboats to carry fishing nets and lines, as well as signalling rockets, flares, a device for the purification of sea water, concentrated fruit juice, tinned milk and a comprehensive medical kit, all secured in such a way that it would be impossible for them to be stolen or lost overboard if the boat capsized. Frederick Grossmith had found, through the Marine Safety Agency in Southhampton, that some of her suggestions became standard in lifeboats around the world. All food, water and equipment are now stowed in secure lockers, and fishing rods are compulsory. Amazingly, though, it's still only an option for lifeboats to carry water purifying equipment. How different our dreadful voyage would have been if we'd been able to convert sea water into fresh!

Grossmith's research also tied up some loose ends that had been nagging at me for years. The American aircraft that had bombed U-156 was a B-24 Liberator, which had flown to the area of the sinking from Ascension Island. The pilot was Lieutenant James Harden who, on discovering the U-boat on the surface towing lifeboats crowded with survivors, radioed back to Ascension asking what action he should take. He was ordered to sink the vessel.

I was also pleased to learn from Grossmith's book that Fred Eyres, *Laconia*'s pantry-man, had survived. But I was shocked to read that 1782 of her passengers ultimately perished.

Grossmith had also interviewed my old shipmate Johnny Hennessey, who told of swimming for 24 hours before, most astonishing of all, being rescued by the crew of U-156. So Johnny had been on the crowded casing of the submarine with many other survivors while Davey Jones and I were down below. Johnny also spoke pleasantly with Hartenstein and, like me, had to swim for his life after the German commander ordered us all overboard when the B-24 attacked.

From a newspaper article I read about Mary, the lovely, gentle woman who died in such a dignified way in our lifeboat. She was in fact Lady Grizel Wolfe-Murray, daughter of the Earl of Glasgow. I now believe that she kept her true identify from us to avoid preferential treatment.

In 2000, I met a former merchant seaman, Captain John Fisher, in Adelaide. When I mentioned that I was a *Laconia* survivor, he told me he knew someone living in Tasmania who also survived the sinking and endured a lifeboat voyage to Africa. This turned out to be Tony Large, a retired doctor who served in the Royal Navy Volunteer Reserve. Incredibly, just a few months before *Laconia* was torpedoed, Tony had also managed to survive the sinking of HMS *Cornwall*. After *Laconia* went down, he found himself in one of the lifeboats that was eventually rounded up by Hartenstein and towed behind U-156. Cast adrift after the American bombing attack, his boat set course for West Africa with 51 men aboard. After a harrowing voyage that lasted an agonising 40 days, Tony was one of just four survivors.

Tony and I exchanged letters, through which I learnt that he had written a book about his experience. He then put me in touch with Ron Croxton, another survivor living in England who, I quickly realised, was the young RAF chap who had been lying in the bow with Doris and me when I first sighted the African coast. He had also been badly traumatised when he realised that people were being forced overboard. The anguish of that voyage had never left him. Interestingly, he had remained in contact with Doris until two or three years before her death in 1991.

When he last saw her she was living in a nursing home and in good spirits, although by then confined to a wheelchair. Ron was also able to tell me that one of the Dutchmen who had so gently looked after us in his home when we were in Grand Bassa was J C Gourdsward.

Miraculously, Ron had been in contact with Harold Gibson, also still living in England. Harold had been a member of our Royal Navy contingent aboard *Laconia*. Indeed, it was Harold who had cried out 'One of ours here!' before hauling me aboard the lifeboat after my exhausting swim from U-156. Harold and I exchanged pleasant letters and telephone calls in which we talked of our ordeal. He recalled pulling people into the lifeboat before the voyage began but had no recollection of saving me specifically.

He also put me onto a video documentary about the *Laconia* sinking and our survival. I obtained a copy from the producer, Nigel Turner, in London. Harold, Ron and Tony were interviewed, clearly still deeply emotional about those long-ago events. Harold, in particular, spoke of suspecting people were put over the side in a desperate bid to save water for those who appeared stronger. I was comforted by the fact that I wasn't alone in not being able to forget those terrible things so long after the event.

In viewing the documentary, I saw for the first time James Harden, the B-24 pilot who bombed U-156. His pain was obvious as he related his role in the whole affair and I think it is terribly sad that he has had to live his life knowing that, by doing his duty, he added to our misery. Like all of us who went through this experience, he remains a prisoner of dreadful memories.

The waves from the sinking of *Laconia* eventually reached the Nuremberg War Trials. As a result of Harden's attack on U-156, Admiral Karl Donitz issued what has since become known as the Laconia Order. The highly respected commander-in-chief of German U-boats instructed that:

1. *No attempt of any kind must be made to rescue members of ships sunk and this includes picking up persons in the water, putting them in lifeboats, righting capsized lifeboats and handing over food and water. Rescue runs counter to the most primitive demands of warfare for the destruction of enemy ships and crews.*

2. *Orders to bring in captains and chief engineers of enemy ships remain in force.*

3. *Shipwrecked people will only be rescued if their information is important for the submarine.*

4. *Be hard. Remember the enemy has no regard for women and children when he bombs German cities.*

At Nuremberg, Donitz's defence counsel pointed out that navies of the Allied nations had also conducted their operations at sea under similar codes of unrestricted warfare. This did not sway the court, which sentenced Donitz to 10 years imprisonment, in part because of his uncompromising wording of the Laconia Order.

I often reflect on the appalling losses at sea suffered by both sides during World War Two. Hundreds of thousands of people lost their lives. Aside from the professional naval personnel, many of those lost were women and children, prisoners of war, the sick and injured, and the civilian crews of merchant supply ships.

It was insanity on a scale that still chills me to the core. Germany's submariners faced daunting odds. At Nuremberg, Donitz revealed that every man in his submarine fleet knew that he would very likely take part in only two patrols before losing his life. The Admiral stated that more than 650 U-boats were sunk and, out of the 40,000 men in the submarine force, 30,000 did not return. Hartenstein and the crew of U-156 were lost on their fifth patrol.

So that's the story of my small part in all that madness at sea long ago. I don't know why I survived while countless others didn't. Some might say it was just the luck of the draw, something to be put down to fate and the apparent random nature of life. As a man of faith, however, I believe otherwise.

Acknowledgements

A number of people have played important roles in helping to bring my story to the surface over the last 10 years. In particular I thank Professor Peter Liddle, for his encouragement and gentle insistence; Nicholas and Eveleen Kerr, for expanding on my brief original account; Lynn Riley, for her enthusiasm and encouragement; Eric Wisgard, for reading early drafts of the manuscript with a journalist's eye and making valued suggestions on structure and style; fellow survivors Harold Gibson and Ron Croxton in England and Tony Large in Tasmania, for their correspondence and recollections; and the late Reverend Frederick Grossmith, for his masterly research and writing on the *Laconia* sinking.

Thanks are also due to Don and Josie Maddern, who put me in touch with Captain John Fisher, who in turn enabled me to connect with Tony Large; to Nigel Turner in London, for his revealing video production; to Chris Gibb, for her checking of the manuscript, candid comments and constant encouragement; and to Dennis Taylor, for his thoughtful appraisal. Also, my grateful and heartfelt thanks to David Gibb, for his hours of patient listening, questioning and writing, without which this book would not have been possible. I extend, too, my thanks and appreciation to Ryan Paine and Michael Bollen at Wakefield Press, for their belief in the value of my story and their insightful editing. Finally, and especially, thanks to all the members of the McLoughlin family who, in countless and wonderful ways, have helped this survivor of war to survive the peace.

J.M.